I0139321

JOURNEY HOMEWARD

Stages Along the Way

●

by

Michael Calvin Braswell

WIPF & STOCK · Eugene, Oregon

Wipf and Stock Publishers
199 W 8th Ave, Suite 3
Eugene, OR 97401

Journey Homeward
Stages Along the Way
By Braswell, Michael
Copyright©1990 by Braswell, Michael
ISBN 13: 978-1-5326-5233-2

Publication date 5/29/2018
Previously published by Franciscan Herald Press, 1990

This book is dedicated to Patrick O'Doherty.

Though a brief encounter,

kindred spirits still.

ACKNOWLEDGMENTS

Although there are a number of persons, past and present, whom I would like to acknowledge, several deserve special mention.

First, there is my grandmother who introduced me in my wide-eyed, younger years to the all-encompassing great sense of mystery found in every nook and cranny of living and dying. More recently, special thanks to my friend, Morton, who helped me to let this book become a basis for deepening our personal friendship as well as our larger spiritual journey. To Steve who read each word I wrote, offering suggestions and encouragement. To Neil and Carol for going the extra mile in helping me find a publisher. To Frederick Buechner for writing an encouraging note. To my wife, Susan, for supporting my dreams and typing my manuscript. And to my two sons, Scott and Matt, for helping me to keep things in perspective.

Thanks also go to my parents, Martha and Calvin, for wanting to be my friends as well as parents and to M. L. To my brothers whom I am almost always glad to see: Steve, Mark, Craig and Lindsey. To Aunt Sara and Laura. To teachers past: Jean, John (and Cleo), Jim, and Reverend Leroy. To friends present who have helped me along the Way, particularly with some aspect of this current work: Bo, Bill, Richard, Allen, Larry, John, Roger, Lon, and Dennis.

Thanks also to Fr. Brinkman, his staff and Hannah Harris for their help.

CONTENTS

FOREWORD

This story is about persons and community. It is about our personal journeys and the journeys of the visible and invisible community of which we are a part.

There are stages we find ourselves experiencing along our way to God. Mystery, a sense of new beginning, crossroad experiences, suffering and transcendence are stages that challenge us time and again as we search for a closer relationship with the one we seek. Our pilgrimage is not linear but more of a spiral toward God, for we re-experience these stages in many forms and shapes throughout our lives. From the wide-eyed awe of my nine-year old eyes and ears as they were held spellbound by the stories from a revered grandmother to the birth of my children to the grief of death stealing unresolved relationships, mystery teaches and reminds me as it does each of us, that within the way there are many paths which I will have to walk.

Finally, it is my hope that this story is about coming as well as going. Coming home to ourselves and the God we seek; the spirit within expressed in the world without; the unfolding of our hearts in fuller relationship with the continuing revelation we seek. It is a journey worth taking. It is the only dance there is.

1

EXPERIENCING THE MYSTERY

"The wind blows where it wills, and you hear the sound of it, but you do not know whence it comes or whither it goes; so it is with everyone who is born of the Spirit." (John 3:8)

Living and dying and all that goes on in between is a mystery to most of us. The way we live our lives, including our relationships with each other, remain for the most part a mystery. Young children seem better able to accept the importance and nature of mystery than do adults. A rock, stick, or piece of wrapping paper, each offers an example of ways children explore the mysteries of their experiences with few, if any, ulterior motives. Chief Standing Bear remembered when children were taught to sit still and enjoy mystery. "They were taught to use their organs of smell, to look when there was apparently nothing to see, and to listen intently; when all seemingly was quiet. A child who cannot sit still is a half-developed child."[1] Perhaps we need to become reacquainted with mystery. Not in a naive or isolated sense, but within the course of our daily lives. An unexpected smile or other act of generosity, an opportunity to fill someone else's need, actually noticing something of beauty,or remembering a special time, all offer examples of becoming more aware of life's mysteries. Of course, to become more aware, we will have to learn to pay attention, and paying attention requires that we, like the children of Chief Standing Bear's village, "be still." Being still is not easy in our fast-food, remote controlled world. Yet, if we do not learn to be still, we cannot listen to the sounds without or hear the voice within us.

Experiencing and growing with a sense of mystery is a basic requirement of finding the sacredness of our own lives; the deeper place that is within each of us which extends to the power that is beyond us. This special place is the essential part of our ground of being, and depends upon our remaining open to and nurturing a continuing experience of mystery. Without the awe and wonder of the sacred, we have only ourselves—our own self-interests—to worship. An example of such self-worship is demonstrated in the following questions: When preparing for a time of worship, am I more concerned with having an open heart and mind or with how I will look to others in my "Sunday Best"? When I am called upon to pray am I communicating with God or performing for the congregation? Apart from our relating to God, we have no personal source of ultimate accountability for what we try to do with our lives. In such a world, we may come to believe that we are responsible only to ourselves and the community of which we are a part rather than to the God of the timeless, which includes the continuum of the past, present, and future. Unless the sacred mystery is inherent in our search for God, we may live with the illusion that we are not ultimately accountable for what we do.

The Mystery of Paradox

Before we can experience the mystery, we must

acknowledge the paradox of our own lives. Paradox informs us that life is often not what it appears to be. We see much of life "through a glass darkly." Sometimes that sure-fire investment of our time, money, or love fails and what was supposed to be cause for a celebration becomes a time of mourning. On other occasions, when life looks its bleakest, everything seems to somehow work out for the better. We have no guarantees, yet we continue to look for them. There was a popular television commercial which suggested that a prudent person should get a "piece of the rock" from a well-known insurance company. That appears to be precisely what we attempt to do— to acquire insurance from the paradoxical, unpredictable whims of life. Looking without for such temporal security is inadequate to say the least. Such insurance always comes after-the-fact and at the cost of our losing something of this world—namely, our car or even our life. The alternative "rock" comes from the interior spaces of our heart, from the temple within which is the grounding for our experience with God. This piece of the rock also costs us something— whether it be our egos or our will. A unique feature of this cost is that it is a price which must be "freely" paid. The one choice is external and temporal, the other is internal and eternal. The choosing is ours to do, whether we want to or not. The mystery is the grace through which we can make such a choice and often losing our way, can return to the way and actually find ourselves. God does not always use "Federal Express." Sometimes the faster we read, the less we comprehend. Sometimes the quicker we get to where we are going, the less certain we are of where we have come from. Sometimes the harder we try to do something, we find, paradoxically, that we are less effective in accomplishing our task.

The paradox of our own life seems to tell us that right and wrong, good and bad, may often be matters of degree, rather than absolutes. Is it absolutely wrong to kill someone? What if that someone is threatening the life of a loved one? Could it still be wrong to take another life, yet be a choice under certain circumstances that we would willingly make? Can a legal act be immoral or an immoral act, legal? Issues ranging from slavery to cheating on one's income tax beg such questions. To put such paradox in a more spiritual perspective, what does it mean if I attend my church regularly and actively participate in its programs, yet engage in unethical or other questionable business practices? What if I neglect my family emotionally in order to assure them of financial security? Can I, in fact, eventually expect to "reap what I sow"? Can I convince myself that God is "up there" doing his thing which leaves me free "down here" to do my thing? After all, I go to church with reasonable regularity and give God his due. After all, my church is the biggest, oldest, or whatever, which must mean it's the best. What could be more important than being number one for God? Matthew writes "But many that are first will be last, and the last first."[2] It seems that while sitting in attractive stained glass buildings we often confuse talk about God and the historical Jesus with experiencing God and that which is sacred or holy. Is God's house more clearly the inspiring Gothic cathedral or the parched desert sky of a starving Africa?

It is mysterious that the more we give of ourselves in relationships, the more we seem to get in return. There is a fair measure of pain to be sure. Still, caring enough to put someone else's needs before my own seems to somehow raise me out of my own skin and add to the quality of my life—even when substantial personal sacrifices may be required. Perhaps that is what the grace of children offers us; a compelling opportunity to think of and care for someone else— someone who truly needs to receive our time and attention as much as we need to give it. One of the

4

great mysteries of children is that they keep the child in each of us alive.

Sometimes we are inclined to believe that if we do not risk anything, at least we will not lose anything, at least we will be able to hold onto what we have. However, the truth appears to be if I risk nothing, I lose everything. This interpersonal paradox is at the center of our relationship with each other and with God. It is not easy to risk my fear of being known by another. It is even more difficult to risk trusting, for betrayal will from time to time be the price for such trust. And finally, there is even the even greater risk of trusting a force that is both within and beyond me that can accept and love me in areas that I cannot accept, in ways that are beyond my conception. It is often hard to remember that no matter how talented I may be or how hard I try, I can do nothing "for" God. Yet, through me the realization of God's purposes may be limitless. Do I only get to keep what I give away? In love's name the answer is yes.

Asking Questions

Asking questions more than coming up with answers moves us toward experiencing the mystery. Frederick Buechner writes, "You do not solve the mystery, you live the mystery."[3] As far as the sacred mystery is concerned, the journey may be more important than the destination.

In a very real sense life is an open-ended question. Asking questions seems more helpful when I have some idea regarding what I "want" to do with the answer. At the center of a questioning heart is the willingness to "listen" for an answer, an answer to provide one with a direction rather than solution. Such an answer avoids the illusion of absolutely solving problems and instead guides one along the way toward the light from beyond. Such a notion is reminiscent of what an old country preacher once said about his ideas on heaven and hell: "I don't know much about it. . . . My guess is that when you die, you will find whatever you were looking for while you were alive." Perhaps his idea regarding the afterlife is true in the present life. The idea of self-fulfilling prophecies and attitudes has been frequently examined by religion, philosophy, and psychology. If my heart is "where I lay up my treasures," then my spiritual search for God may be more closely connected to my automobile, house, or television set than to my temple within. If my primary sanctuary for worship is the front seat of my Cadillac or the recliner in front of my television set, then where is the god for whom I am looking? Some may call it idolatry while others may call it success. After all, God does help those who help themselves—or is it others? Is searching for God in such a direction justified if we are really trying to "win one for the eternal gipper"? Certainly, many warlords throughout the eons of history have thought so. Do I really have to lose myself to God's purposes in order to find myself? Is "Cadillac Christianity" a legitimate way to God, or is it little more than the symbolic handwashing of a Pontius Pilate concerning my and others' spiritual needs? Perhaps in some strange way, it is all a part of our journey along the way; the pragmatic Pilate and the suffering servant each laying claim to our soul. Perhaps it is more a question of the "quality" of our spiritual struggle which is essential to nurturing our sense of wonder and mystery.

The core of the questioning life depends upon "priorities"—the importance which we attribute to what we spend our time looking for, to what we worship. Our time and our energy are our most important resources, and it is by how much time and energy we spend doing whatever we do that we can measure what is most important to us. Time, of course, refers

6

to the quantity of minutes and hours we commit to an experience. Energy, however, is more concerned with our attitude toward the experiences to which we are committing our time. Do I have a creative attitude that engenders hope in the unseen possibilities of a particular experience or am I simply "doing time"? Rollo May once wrote, "Psychologically and spiritually man does not live by the clock alone. His time, rather, depends on the significance of the event."[4] At the center of our questioning, our search for God is also a search for significance and meaning in our own lives.

When counseling couples or families, I have heard husbands and wives refer to the "quality" time they spend with each other and their children in reference to the significance and meaning of their family life. The idea seems to suggest that while not much time is spent with the loved ones in question, at least it is quality time. However, the truth seems to be more of the nature that to a large extent, "all" time is quality time, be it poor or good. At issue in defining quality time is: do I spend *enough* time with my loved ones? This notion seems to be as much a measure of quality as anything else. There is no doubt that many husbands and wives work long hours to provide for each other and their children. Yet there is also little doubt that sharing non-special as well as special time is required for intimacy and closeness to evolve. This is true in our relationships with each other and with God. The child playing in the yard, knowing that a loving parent while not seen is as close as the sound of his or her voice, feels a unique sense of security. And so it is with a child of God.

If asking questions is to be of any help in providing us with spiritual direction, we must try (not necessarily always succeed) to be honest in our questioning. The idea of quality time when taken to its exaggerated and trendy extreme, appears to be an excellent example of how we often fool ourselves for a while or at least justify the misery of our own misplaced priorities. It is as a close friend once said to me in a moment of reflection, "You start out running your business and your business ends up running you." An even more poignant thought along this line of thinking is reflected in the comment, "How many people do you know who when they come to the end of their lives wish that they had more time to spend with their business?"[5] Since the way we spend our time and energy is critical to how we arrange our priorities, we need to carefully consider what is really important to us.

Sometimes we find an inverse relationship between how we spend our time and energy, and what is most important to us. I may often spend the least time and energy with that which I feel is most important to me. I may think that my spouse and children are most important to me, but in reality the bulk of my time and energy may be spent on 60-80 hour work weeks in pursuit of my career. Asking questions such as who am I? where am I going? and why? can help me better understand what my priorities really are as opposed to what I often think they are. This process can also help clarify what God or gods I am genuinely seeking.

Parables and Mystery

Parables provide the questioning heart with an important pathway through which one can gain insight into the mysteries of life, including its paradoxical nature. Whether Aesop's fables or the example of the mustard seed, parables use simple stories to illustrate significant moral and spiritual issues as well as provide us with an invitation into the mysterious. Perhaps most importantly, parables offer us a way to overcome the limits of language in discovering mystery—the spirit of the message. The parable offers us a hint of the infinite within the context of the finite, the timeless within the restraint of our limited sense of time. As an acorn has the potential to become a towering oak or a helpless infant the possibility of becoming a powerful social force as an adult, the parable provides us with a glimpse into the mystery of the future extended from the realities of the present.

Parables always seem to contain a quality of hiddenness or concealment, much as the promise of the oak is concealed within the husk of an acorn or a lowly birth in a Bethlehem manger hides the promise of a Messiah. The truth of parables, if nothing else, should encourage us to be more humble, for things will not always be as they presently seem to be. Parable images direct us to the extraordinary possibilities of our ordinary world, one day at a time; images of sowing and reaping, the vineyard, or fig tree. Each birth offers us the concealed mystery of another chance for ourselves and our world, be it hope or despair, a Hitler or a Gandhi. The animals, trees, all of nature herald the mysteries of God's nature. Such reminders can help keep God's charge of stewardship over his domain at the center of our being. Yet, our memories fade as we listen to the sounds of the world and its progress. Such progress encourages us to disdain the powers of the more primitive spirit and contributes to our loss of spiritual balance. On rare occasions, such as a ride through the mountains during the fall season or a sunset walk along a deserted seashore, may bring forth a brief sigh of recognition. Still, for the most part, we choose to allow ourselves little time to hear such voices. We think we want less mystery in our lives, not more. We are inclined to settle for the illusion of certainty, rather than face the uncertainty of the mysterious. Perhaps we need to recapture the wondering spirit of children in order that we may more fully listen to the transcendent truths of the parable as a way to experiencing mystery.

The Mystery of Love

Love may well be the ultimate mystery. People do horrible and wonderful things to each other in the name of love. While we have great difficulty in defining love, we spend the greater part of our lives searching for it. "God is love."[6] What does that mean? Doing good to those who are trying to hurt you does not seem to make any kind of real sense. If God is love, why does he let bad things happen to us? The potential for such questioning seems endless. As human beings the best we seem to be able to hope for is to look for justice tinged with a dash of mercy (but only for those we feel are deserving). If we cannot love, perhaps we can be just. Maybe we can even create laws, rules, and so forth to ensure justice for everybody, even criminals. We are also inclined to apply that same line of thinking to God with our visions of heaven and hell. Yet in a deeper, quieter place, we may experience a hint that the mystery of God's love, including to whatever extent it is reflected in our own lives, is much more than justice. Job's meeting with God describes the overwhelming nature of such an experience. Then Job answered the Lord, and said, "I know thou canst do all things, and that no purpose of thine can be thwarted. . . . I had heard of thee by the hearing of the ear, but now my eye sees thee; therefore I despise myself and repent in dust and ashes."[7] Within the "awesome" context of Old Testament accounts of God, the New Testament teachings of Jesus created a new tapestry—God's "abiding love" for his creation. A terrible love in its suffering, yet finally a transcending love in its power to reconcile all of life's circumstances.

Job's quest for justice became irrelevant when he experienced the overwhelming presence of God.

God's presence as LOVE does more than "kiss and make it well." The pathway or bridge that evolves from our looking and his waiting becomes a meeting place for his presence; a presence that reconciles this world and the timeless, the spirit and the body. God's love and presence makes the price of our experience, however painful or joyful it may be, worth paying. Most of us are not inclined to look for God as honestly, diligently, or as creatively as Job did. Still, we have examples in our relationships with each other that point the way to God. The signposts are there, whether or not we choose to follow them.

As love is the ultimate mystery, it is also the ultimate paradox. Love is simultaneously the most powerful and powerless force. "It is the most powerful because it alone can conquer that final and most impregnable stronghold which is the human heart. It is the most powerless because it can do nothing except by consent."[8] The capacity and ability to receive and give love is the fundamental gift or God's grace. An important part of love's mystery is that it must be received before it can be given. If it was but a matter of the mind, love could be learned from a book. But it is not; it must be experienced. The experience of love requires the attention of mind, body, and spirit. Without love, nothing else really seems to matter very much. The criminal psychopath learns at an early age that people are not to be trusted and that life is essentially a "bad joke." Severe emotional neglect and inconsistent rearing practices as a child encourage the psychopath to become an interpersonal chameleon. Quick and flexible adaption to changing emotional climates become a requirement for survival. I may be punished today for what I was rewarded for yesterday. I can trust no one nor depend on any circumstance. Beaten and bruised emotionally and physically, I learn that the world is a dangerous place so I must become a dangerous person. I am an alien to the possibilities of a reconciling love. Love requires conscience—a sense of responsibility. Without a conscience, the psychopath is free from the rules of society, yet trapped within the despair of not having access to love's liberation.

While the lack of love is mysterious in its potential for the dark and destructive side of human personality, the act of love is no less mysterious in its ability to sustain and nurture the miracle of life. The feeding of the hungry, the reclamation of the reclusive spinster, the welcome birth of the infant, all dance to the rhythm of love. The example several years ago of an insurance salesman putting others on a rescue helicopter ahead of himself after an airplane crash into an icy Potomac river is an example in a human context of Christ's "giving himself, a ransom for many." Why did he do it? He certainly was not expected to make such a sacrifice. After all, he was an insurance salesman, no one special. The human thing to do would have been to save himself. He would have still been a hero, since he had already rescued several of the passengers. During a later news interview, the helicopter pilot gave a moving account of the salesman's assisting one after another of the floundering passengers onto the rescue craft. Eye to eye with the unlikely hero, the pilot felt certain that the salesman realized that he would not survive the time it took the helicopter to deliver the next-to-last passenger to safety and return for him. What made him decide in those final crucial seconds to die so that the others might live? There was no time for goodbyes to family and friends, there was only the moment and the choice it offered. What thoughts passed through his final moments of consciousness; the smiling faces of his wife and children at a July 4th picnic? An unfinished business report? A lingering regret for a past indiscretion? Or the warm embrace of a loving grandparent? Whatever they were, we know that he "drank of the cup," but we really do not know why. Although we are saddened by his passing, in a strange way we are glad he made the choice. His act of love reminds us, as have other such sacrifices, of the power and grace the human spirit is capable of when responding to the love and power which is beyond us. It does not make much sense, but still it is there, usually just out of our reach. Perhaps during that split second of eternity he joined Job in experiencing the mystery of God's presence and love. If he did, nothing else really mattered and we, along with his family, have been left with a legacy far greater than any other success he could have shared with us.

Endnotes

1. Whitehall N. Perry, *A Treasury of Traditional Wisdom* (New York: Simon & Schuster, 1971), p. 989.
2. Matthew 19:30
3. Frederick Buechner, *Wishful Thinking* (New York: Harper & Row, 1973), p. 64.
4. Rollo May, *Man's Search For Himself* (New York: Norton, 1953), p. 220.
5. Anonymous
6. 1 John 4:16
7. Job 42: 2; 5-6
8. Frederick Buechner, *Wishful Thinking*, pp. 53-54.

2

BEGINNING THE JOURNEY

"Go your way; behold, I send you out as lambs in the midst of wolves." (Luke 10:3)

"He alone is God who can never be sought in vain: not even when he cannot be found." (St. Bernard of Clairvaux)

"Beginning the Journey" may not be a completely accurate way of discussing the time in our lives when we begin to purposefully seek God. From birth, we are on the journey whether we are fully aware of it or not. Perhaps all of life's experiences contribute to whatever point we have come to in our seeking. Even if our searching has led us away from God, the invitation to come home still follows our every move. Perhaps we can never completely escape from the mercy of the God who is love and will not leave without us.

Yet there is a beginning in which we are required to struggle with all that we are, both our dark side that hides from the light and the small voice of hope that desires relationships with the love that is beyond us. It may be more accurate to identify our "beginning" the journey as the moment in our existence when we

14

become aware that we are, in fact, on life's journey. Our seeking can then become less mindless and more mindful as we attempt to respond to the compelling nature of the Holy Spirit.

We all journey through life. We are born, grow up, get married, and spend our time doing whatever we do. Sometimes we are more aware of the course of our lives, sometimes less. Major events—marriage, the birth of our children, the death of loved ones—provide us with primary reference points or maps from which we may or may not try to alter the paths which we have chosen. During much of our journey we do not seem to be very aware of where we are going or why we are going there. Sometimes we find ourselves moving in circles; or just when we thought we were finally accomplishing some sought after goal, reaching a dead end. Yet strangely enough, as haphazard as our wandering may be, it often all seems worth it. It just seems so hard to remember what is really important in our life's journey. We appear to spend so much of our energy on wealth instead of wisdom, the inventory of our property instead of our hearts. Still, all of life's experiences, one way or another, can be an important part of our going to God.

This chapter is primarily concerned with our consciously choosing to try to remember our way along the spiritual path. Once we have become reacquainted with a sense of mystery; we can again make a choice, one that we are conscious of and more responsive to. For we can then begin to realize that as in our relationships to each other, our relationship to God requires our time and energy—our attention—if we are to know joy and peace in the deepest part of our being. As we begin to re-experience the wonder and mystery of relationship, we find ourselves returning to our own beginnings in search of reconciling the contradictions of our own personal histories, the good and the bad that each of us experiences. For the journey we now wish to consciously resume started long ago in another land that does not have to be so faraway.

In The Beginning

Upon birth the security of the womb is abruptly interrupted by competing smells, textures, and visions, all of which bring with them varying degrees of pleasure and pain, closeness and separation, hope and despair. The infant grows into a world full of expectations— from being cute and lovable to being a good or bad little boy or girl. Personal history emerges from the web of family history both seen and unseen. Genetics and experience dictate no more or no less. The remembered sounds and smells of long ago summer evenings spent with my grandmother on her small dusty front porch are inextricably woven into the fabric of my own growing-up days. These times, as do the particular times of each of us, provide important reference points on the maps of our personal journeys. Such memories seem as much as anything else to give us our unique sense of personal history with which we increasingly identify as we grow older. If our identities are to develop in a healthy, balanced way, we must experience an adequate share of love from those we depend on. A modern tragedy we must reckon with in our land of plenty is that more children may go to bed hungry for love than with stomachs empty of food. Child abuse and suicide statistics as well as increasing numbers of juvenile offenders indicate that a primary element which is essential to the development of healthy, hopeful children is missing in many lives.

The lesson of love is a lesson that must be received before it can be given. No matter how many self-help books I read, I cannot learn "how to" love myself or anyone else. I must first be loved by others before I can muster up the courage to risk deeply caring for someone else. Sam Keen states it quite succinctly when he says, "I was loved, therefore I am."[1] To extend this notion from an exclusive human perspective to the timeless domain of relating to God, John says, "We love, because he first loved us."[2]

Children who are abused and neglected physically or emotionally are deprived in the deepest part of their being of a sense of love and worth. Unlike healthy children who feel a sense of their own personal value, abused children have no such reference point. As suggested earlier, they can easily become psychological "chameleons," learning to survive by constantly adjusting their personalities and loyalties to the ever-changing whims of maladjusted parents. They survive, rather than grow, in a world of confusing circumstances. Physically they become adults, but because the seed of love has never been planted or nurtured, they remain empty emotionally. Their growing up years are full of pain and inconsistencies. They learn to be loyal only to the moment's opportunities, never to the people involved in their lives. Their relationships teach them early in life that people cannot be trusted and that love will not be available to them no matter what they do or say. As a result they are released from the restraints of conscience, free to manipulate people and circumstances to their own immediate advantage. Unfortunately, they are also isolated from love's intimacy which is a primary basis for life's being worth living. No matter what success they attain, they usually manage to fail in the end. For they have known all along that their destiny was a meaningless one. A pretender to love's gifts and responsibilities, their restless journey ends before it has begun.

Most children begin their life's journey with a different legacy. Although it is true enough that most of us never receive as much love as we feel we need, we all have to receive "enough" to get us started on our way. Eventually we may find ourselves on the way, realizing "our" way is an unnecessary encumbrance. The seed of love is usually planted by our parents, imperfect as they may be. In fact, we may find as we get older that our love for our parents is largely based on our past times together—the sacrifices and mistakes during the laughing-crying crazy world of our childhood. When we needed, they somehow gave. Often what they gave did not seem to be enough, but was usually more than their childhoods gave them. As adults we find we must earn each other's respect. Still, the wellspring of our childhood experience rarely runs dry of the debt we owe our parents. Our parents or other significant others loved us enough to get us started on our particular journey. No matter where life took us or what we did, we would not be abandoned. We would not be alone. There was someone who loved us still. From this nest of emotional security, we could decide when it was safe to take risks—to begin to "fall in love with life." We could experience rejection without the fear of abandonment. We could feel emotional pain with the knowledge that all was not lost—that we would not die. Our loved ones nurtured the seed of our caring for and taking care of ourselves. Scott Peck writes, "For when children know that they are valued, when they truly feel valued in the deepest parts of themselves, then they feel valuable . . . this feeling of being valuable is a cornerstone of self-discipline because when one considers oneself valuable one will take care of oneself in all ways that are necessary."[3] From our storehouse of of love, we find we can begin to explore the intellectual, emotional, and sensual dimensions of ourselves and others. It may well be that we have to fall in love with life before we can fall in love with God. In any event, beginning the journey of life is fueled by the mystery of love's energies. This mystery also invites and guides us toward our journey to God—a journey that allows our love for ourselves and each other to extend to a love that is beyond us, yet nearby, one that we may in time hope to share with our Creator.

Many Voices

Many voices call to us as we get on with our lives. These voices compete for our time and energy. They invite us to invest our physical, emotional, and intellectual nature with their particular promise of fulfillment. From the latest look in fashion to the new gourmet in-food to another therapeutic guru, we heed the call for fulfillment in the here and now—right here and right now. Naive, though well-intentioned, we become intoxicated with our own scent; and, as a result, the aroma of success is often limited to the smell of money or other symbols of success. Overweight physically, intellectually frivolous, and emotionally immature, we are inclined to become the mindless consumer, responding to the short-term "good deal," whether we need it or not, without considering the long-term consequences. Perhaps we should be less concerned with income and more concerned with outcome. In any event, the "bottom line" is where we often find ourselves—responding to the call of the lowest common denominator that emphasizes the quantity and variety of experience rather than quality and depth. Unfortunately the bottom line can also become the bottom-of-the-well. Placing a priority on short-term profits and quick-fix solutions to personal and social problems inhibits our spiritual potential for enlarging our vision—the ability to remain responsive to our immediate needs yet see beyond the nearest horizon to possibilities that are remembered only in our dreams. These many voices can seduce us into believing who we are is somehow dependent on what we have. Appearances become more important than being. The illusion or appearance of salvation encourages us to participate in a spiritual charade—one where we as consumers can buy our salvation.

Every town has its shopping mall. Every town has its cathedral. Every day is a holy day where sacred denominations ranging from Niemann-Marcus to K-Mart demonstrate their piety. With each blue-light special and red-tag sale, they offer you and me another chance to purchase our salvation. Unfortunately our trip to the promised land has a limited warranty—one that expires long before our payments stop. So on we go, following the sound of the nearest (and loudest) voice, looking around every corner for salvation on sale. Those persons who are not compelled to choose an approved brand of such shopping-mall salvation are quickly labeled as lazy, nonproductive, or at best, eccentric. Frederick Buechner refutes such labels when comparing slothfulness and laziness: "Sloth is not to be confused with laziness. A lazy man, a man who sits around and watches the grass grow, may be a man at peace. His sun-drenched, bumblebee dreaming may be the prelude to action or itself an act well worth the acting. A slothful man, on the other hand, may be a very busy man. He is a man who goes through the motions, who flies on automatic pilot. Like a man with a bad head cold, he has mostly lost his sense of taste and smell. He knows something is wrong with him, but not wrong enough to do anything about it. Other people come and go, but through glazed eyes he hardly notices them. He is letting things run their course. He is getting through his life."[4]

The many voices that encourage us to make choices and establish priorities may help us "get through" our life, but they do not necessarily help us grow through our life. Sometimes listening to the many voices makes it difficult to hear the "still small voice" of God. Remembering to listen for the call of the Holy Spirit is not easy. Such listening requires that we develop a different kind of attitude, an attitude that attends to the prevailing mystery and wonder of God. In order to develop such an attitude, we must pursue the "discipline of the spirit."

The Discipline of the Spirit

Paul writes, "where the Spirit of the Lord is, there is freedom."[5] The idea of being liberated sounds promising, especially from a distance. The closer we get to liberation, the less appealing it appears. The glitter of precious stones from afar becomes on closer inspection, a crown of thorns. The diamonds and rubies may come to more clearly resemble blood and tears. Being free also means being responsible. Inherent in responsibility is the ability-to-respond. For the spiritual seeker whose journey to God is becoming more conscious, this response-ability translates into an increasing openness to the Holy spirit, an openness that seeks issue in action. The focus the Holy Spirit provides may guide one toward subtle or more visible action. In any event, this process of liberation can prove to be as unsettling as it is liberating. In the face of such a metamorphosis, it is essential for one to develop a sense of spiritual balance. One way to move toward such balance is through the discipline of the spirit.

It is easier to love people in general or in the abstract than someone you know in particular. One might also add to this notion that it is easier to donate a cashier's check to a worthy cause than to give one's time. Given this fundamental condition of our human hypocrisy, it is still true that we cannot love everyone equally or give ourselves without reservation to every worthy cause. We have only so much time and energy. For most of us, there are only a few persons in our life with whom we will share intimacy, and even these special relationships are vulnerable to becoming

21

trivialized through a variety of recurring habits and rituals. The mandatory Christmas cards, the obligatory birthday necktie, and the Friday night canasta club maintain the habit of our special relationships. The same holds true regarding our relationship to God. Wedding vows, christenings, familiar well-worn pews, the dog-eared pages of favorite hymns, all maintain the sacred traditions and habits of what we perceive as our spiritual relationship to God. However, if we look more closely at our worldly and spiritual habits, we may find that they do not differ as much as we might think.

Christmas cards and candlelight communion and bingo at the church on Friday nights blend into social habits which we attribute to our sense of the sacred. It is true enough that these habits are important and enhance the quality of community life both socially and perhaps at times, spiritually. While such habits are a useful part of our lives, when extended into the lifeblood of the sacred, they may often prove to be more about us and less about God. Needed ministries to the disenfranchised living in another world a few miles across town or a few feet from us in our television sets all too quickly become a distant second priority to the proposed stained glass window or the marble tile for the church foyer. Comfortable traditions are more inclined to be limited to offering comfort for the daily problems of living at the expense of one's spiritual growth which evolves from trying to meet the many faces of human need. These faces include the latch-key children, the homeless, the disabled elderly, the victims of family violence and sexual abuse, and the hungry of the world. Spreading ourselves too thin leaves us little energy to respond to such challenges and invites us to long for the comfort of simply coping. It seems we often start out in life striving to succeed and end up settling for survival. Trying to do more than we have the time and energy to do is nonproductive at best and destructive at worst. Such efforts also encourage us to confuse appearances with reality, the busyness of our lives with the quality of our actions.

Central to the dilemma of our spiritual imbalance is our apparent lack of discipline. A friend once identified this deficiency as arising out of our being "evasive."[6] Our evasiveness moves us to avoid the struggle to meet spiritual challenges. Instead of seeking God, we seek the status-quo of our own self-interests. Our motto might be, "no news is good news." Like Buechner's sloth, we follow the path of least resistance and simply seek to survive the life to which we have been sentenced. We choose obedience over discipline. We follow the many voices from without rather than listen for the still small voice within. We look for orders to follow, authorities to guide us, and groups to belong to. Discipline requires personal response-ability; an internal set of spiritual values that can sustain us in the course of our life's journey, including our experiences of both the peaks and the valleys of living. The obedient person tries to evade the difficult ambiguities in living. The disciplined person tries to engage such ambiguities in an effort to experience reconciliation.

How does the disciplined person come to a point of spiritual balance? While there may be a number of ways, one way is through meditation. Meditation has historically been an important means of spiritual seeking in both eastern and western religions. From practical yogi techniques to Christian contemplative traditions, meditation has enabled seekers to become more disciplined in their search for God. Current psychology and psychotherapy treatments have also utilized meditation not so much as a means of spiritual seeking, but rather as a technique for relaxing mind and body. While secular therapeutic applications of meditation are useful, the intent of sacred applications of meditation seek more than physical and mental relaxation.

Meditation

Meditation provides a way for us to become more liberated through the experience of spiritual balance. John Main writes, ". . . meditation is simply the process whereby we come to terms with these truths: truths about God, truths about ourselves, truths, too, about our neighbor."[7] Main goes on to suggest that meditation activates our spirit. Meditation is not really a rational effort, although thinking about God may be a prelude to such efforts. The meditator attempts to move beyond thought and feeling toward experiencing the power of the Holy Spirit within oneself. Generally speaking, for the person seeking God, this process is grounded in prayer and genuine reflection on one's life; a reflection that unmasks the pretensions of the world's illusions which we take to be real; a reflection that includes the truths of the Scriptures and the ongoing commitment of our communicating with God. In seeking God, we find more of ourselves. As we lose our personal sense of self in consciously choosing to begin our journey to God, we find we must first be able to accept personal responsibility for who we are. In other words, we must first be able to say "I am," before we can say "I am a follower of Christ." As enriching and important as genuine reflection and study of the Scriptures are, the heart of meditation builds on such efforts and seeks to go beyond the self into the center of God's will. It is the difference between thinking about what the relationship with God will be in the "sweet by and by," and beginning to more fully and directly experience relationship with God in the eternal now.

The following are some general suggestions for beginning personal meditation: A "preparation" state often helps one become more mindful of a meditative attitude. Reading Scriptures or listening to quiet, meaningful music can aid in creating an enhanced mood or atmosphere for meditative experience. The "meditation" stage is, of course, at the center of spiritual discipline. A "special word" or mantra may be selected to concentrate on. In fact, meditation could be referred to as a state of "relaxed concentration." The purpose of meditation is to clear one's mind so that the individual can more clearly hear the "still small voice" and become more receptive to the Holy Spirit. One might choose the English word, Jesus, or perhaps the Aramaic words *maranatha* (come quickly, Lord Jesus) or *abba* (father) which Jesus himself spoke. Of course, there are a number of other special words which the seeker may choose. Once the "special word" has been chosen, commitment to an established schedule of meditation is essential if one is to receive the benefits of meditation. Some simple rules: 1) Find a special, quiet "place in which to meditate; 2) Find a "time" to meditate when the area is quiet and there are no distractions, preferably twice daily. Persons often schedule their meditation early in the morning at the beginning of their day and during the evening at the end of their day. 3) Try to meditate for a designated period of time during each meditation experience. It is usually recommended that beginning meditators set aside at least twenty minutes for each session. It seems important to note that for beginners, the "discipline" of one's meditating every day is more important than when or how long one meditates. 4) Some persons meditate sitting on the floor (usually on a pillow) with legs crossed. However, many less limber seekers find it just as satisfactory to sit in a straight-backed chair. Regardless of one's sitting arrangements, it is important to keep the spine as straight as possible. 5) For the designated period, the person silently repeats the special word. Over and over again the special word is silently sounded out in one's mind and heart. There will be distractions, particularly in the form of other thoughts. Such is the nature of meditation. Whenever one becomes aware of such distraction he or she should simply "return" to the special word. The "only" requirement is that one repeat the special word.

Besides the preparation and meditation stages, one may also find it rewarding to sit quietly for a few moments following the meditation experience. This quiet time can allow the experience to be savored and prepare one to resume the day's or evening's activities, refreshed and more open to the Spirit's presence. Of course, there are also other forms of meditation. Whatever the form, at the center of the disciplined spirit, sought through the experience of meditation, is a questioning heart.

More on the Questioning Heart

It seems true enough that as we grow older we want to find answers we can depend on. Unanswered questions are more than a little troubling. They add ambiguity to our search for a more simplified life of certainty. Safe knowledge is preferred over new knowledge: the convenient alternative over what really needs to be done. We want to view people and events as right or wrong, good or bad, rather than as some of both. It can be frustrating to realize that I, or my group, or my country can be both right and wrong, good and bad; that it is a matter of degree rather than an exclusive absolute. On some occasions what may be good for me may be bad for you, or at least take place at your expense; that in some crazy way we are all in it together—all the little children and adults, red, yellow, black, and white. The evening oracle known as television repeats the message over and over, night after night, that we do reap what we, as well as others, sow. As far as most of life's questions are concerned, each person must answer for him or herself. And the answers, whether individual or collective, always ask new questions which themselves demand to be answered. And so it goes, questions of various sorts and colors hiding behind every answer we arrive at. Whatever happened to the "good old days" when life was simpler? When a man's word was his bond?

As we get older we often try to return to that mythical time when life was simple—simple truth and simple justice. We insulate our homes and hearts—our exteriors and interiors—from the questions as best we can. The sounds of hunger and need are not "easy listening" and cry out ever louder as we evade them and withdraw to an increasingly narrow space. Our openness to such questions diminishes as our minds and hearts become more restricted. Of course, it was not always this way. Whatever happened to the unfulfilled questions of our youth? The mad, happy energy that reached for dreams barely seen and mostly imagined? Intelligence and innocence emerging into a newfound awareness of the way things are supposed to be, demanding change no matter how impractical. Personal, national, international, even universal wrongs must be made right—now! Promises made within the protests of the fleeting magic of youth awakening into adulthood. Our youth held forth so much promise for us; yet as adults we have settled for so much less.

In the beginning of our journey to God, we have a hint of a vision. With heads tilted slightly, we listen for the subtle sounds of a familiar melody. Our senses are more alert and there is a forgotten scent of anticipation in the air.

We have been for the most part asleep until now. Now our eyes are open and although our vision is less than perfect, we are aware of the continuing invitation to come closer to that which we long for. We are finally happy just to know more fully that we are on our way, no matter how misguided or inarticulate our travels may occasionally be.

Endnotes

1. Sam Keen, *The Passionate Life* (San Francisco: Harper & Row, 1983), p. 36.
2. 1 John 4:19
3. Scott Peck, *The Road Less Traveled* (New York: Simon & Schuster, 1978), p. 24.
4. Frederick Buechner, *Wishful Thinking* (new York: Harper & Row, 1973), p. 89.
5. II Corinthians 3:17
6. A conversation with Morton Brown
7. John Main, *Christian Meditation* (Montreal: Benedictine Priory, 1982), p. 27.

3

CHOSEN PATHS

"Before man are life and death, whichever he chooses shall be given him." (Ecclesiasticus 15:17)
What a man does here and now with holy intent is no less important, no less true—being a . . . link with Divine Being—than the life in the world to come." (Martin Buber)

Once we have experienced the mystery of God's grace and have become aware of our ongoing spiritual journey, we begin to become more sensitive to the pathways we choose. It is true enough that there are many aspects of our existence that we do not choose —the color of our eyes, the kind of world we will be born into, whether or not it will rain, and so on. Most of us experience our share of good fortune and mis-fortune. Within the arena of life's experiences, both chosen and unchosen, we give life meaning as best we can. Sometimes we get confused. Sometimes we confuse a bulging stock portfolio with personal security, the wailing of Dachau with the pride of a national anthem, and a "piece of the rock" with peace of mind. As we make our choices, large and small, we say we want what is rightfully ours, our fair share, what we deserve: Yet like the prodigal son, we seek the glitter of the inheritance which often turns out to be fool's gold; and the consequences of choices made often smell of the despair of being lost with no hope of finding our way back to the love that we left all too quickly. Still, over time, we stumble back, bruised and broken, to a place we remember in our dreams; the timeless smile from a faded snapshot; the outstretched arms of a waiting father with a warm robe and heart to match; or a star over a Bethlehem manger.

Even as we renew the struggle to make more meaningful choices and find our way, the contradictions remain. We are still inclined to want what we want when we want it. We mask our tendency to search for fool's gold with high-minded slogans and social chatter. A popular song raising millions for famine relief becomes yesterday's news and falls from its number one position on the music charts, carrying with it all the people who supported it who must now look for a shiny new cause. Still, in the parched, despairing heart of Africa, famine is "number one" on the charts. Inherent in our choosing is a fickle sense of the double-standard. More specifically, we demand justice and deliverance when we feel we are the victim and mercy and forgiveness when we are the offender. Yet despite the inconsistency and inadequacy of our choices, we are mercifully not given what we deserve. Why is it that some who have worked so diligently appear to have less than others who have given so little? Why does it sometimes seem that "only the good die young"? Why does life often not seem to "add up"? Who or what is in control of our lives? What, if any, difference does it make?

It seems clear enough that many, if not most, of the choices we make have little or no control over the outcome in events with which we participate. There are no guarantees. Life brings to each of us what it will, both good and bad. The wealthy business man stricken in his prime with an inoperable cancer, the promising career of a ballet dancer ended in the twisted metal of a highway accident, or the bankrupt farmer with the winning lottery ticket, all attest to the unpredictability of life's outcomes. It is true that we live our lives "as if" we were in control and perhaps such play-acting has its own merits in outcomes not seen, yet hoped for. Still, play-acting cannot deliver authentic results. Even if done-by-the-numbers, it cannot make someone love or respect me. Appearances and reality are often not the same. The church with the biggest enrollment may not be the church with the biggest heart. The meaning of the widow's mite though clothed in poverty spoke of riches greater than the eye could see or the mind could imagine. If we cannot control what life brings us through our choices, what can we choose? We can choose how we try to respond to whatever life brings us. Such choosing is an act of our will.

The Fire From Within

Human will has been a longstanding subject of inquiry by Christians and non-Christians alike. Nietzsche's "will to power," Tillich's "courage to be," and Frankl's "will to meaning," all point to the reality that there is a quality inside of us that is always reaching for something more. Frankl writes, ". . . rather than dismissing the concept of a will to meaning as wishful thinking, one could more justifiably conceive of it as a self-fulfilling prophecy."[1] Frankl goes on to describe his experiences in the concentration camps at Dachau and Auschwitz in this context: "Other things being equal, those most apt to survive the camps were those oriented toward the future—toward a task, or a person, waiting for them in the future, toward a meaning to be fulfilled by them in the future."[2] We are not just trying to survive, we are trying to improve our life situation. Our Will wants to expand rather than reduce life's possibilities. Unfortunately, we may often confuse means with meaning. For some of us, our will is directed solely toward the world which is outside of us, the world of things or as Erich Fromm put it, the world of "having" as opposed to "being." For instance, we react to opportunities and manipulate contingencies in an effort to become financially independent. In the end, however, we find that while financial independence may be attained, emotional independence cannot. Such persons use the will as a "means to an end" and often an unsatisfactory end at that. Those of us who have experienced a sense of mystery and have consciously begun our journey are more inclined to respond rather than simply react to the questioning process that is life as we attempt to bring meaning to who we are and where we are going. Interestingly, Frederick Buechner, in discussing the Bible as a way of responding to life's questions, suggests "Don't start looking in the Bible for the answers it gives. Start by listening to the questions it asks."[3] Our responding is what maintains our momentum toward our journey to God and is reflected in the Lord's Prayer—that "his will" be done (in us and through us) on earth as it is in heaven. Perhaps someday we can pay attention long and ardently enough so that his will can become more of our own. As the passing years remind us of missed chances, intended and unintended deceptions, and a variety of other real and imagined hurts, it becomes evident that we cannot do all that much for ourselves, much less carry out to any significant extent God's purposes on our own. Although it turns out that there is really nothing we can do "for" God, the possibilities are unlimited for what God can do "through" us. God does not necesssarily call us to be successful in the eyes of the world. God does not necessarily help those who help themselves (usually they do not feel they need God's help; in fact, they may often claim to speak for God). He calls us to do whatever he calls us to do. The garbage collector or the banker, Mother Teresa or the Hollywood movie star, it makes less difference "what" we are doing than "why" we are doing it. God does not exist to provide us with room service so that we can call on him whenever we need something. He does not serve us. We serve him. And through seeking to serve his purposes, we may find the peace we are searching for. At some point in time, we have to decide that more than anything else we want a relationship with God; we want to become more aware of his way and will deep within us. The critical decision to consciously begin our journey to God must be made over and over again, in good times and bad as our will becomes increasingly enveloped in his own. As an anguished Jesus himself prayed to his Father in the midst of the garden's darkness, "Not as I will, but as thou wilt."[4]

Intentions as Choices

At the active center of our will are our intentions. Our intentions, good or bad, represent our expectations and dreams. As mentioned earlier, we do not control the outcomes of our life's experiences; rather we participate in whatever experiences we are a part of. We are guaranteed nothing. Our fundamental choice, then, consists in how we try to respond to whatever comes our way. Our intentions demonstrate what we are committed to. The accompanying challenge to this reality is that we try to more clearly and consistently articulate with our behavior what our interior life knows to be true. Our intentions are less affected by the consequences of our actions and are more related to our growing sense of awareness and destiny. For the one seeking God, "intentions as choices" reflect our continued efforts of trying to put our good intentions into action without regard to outcome; of trying to more clearly articulate and realize the way of the Holy Spirit in our personal life. An old saying, "the road to hell is paved with good intentions," is only partially true. Good intentions as only thoughts not acted upon produce an immobilizing burden of guilt and fear in one's heart that allows what Scott Peck refers to as "banal evil" to occur.[5] In other words, not acting upon my good intentions may increase the possibilities for someone else to fill the void and choose to act out their bad intentions. That is perhaps why the activities of one's will are never neutral. They either add to or detract from one's personal and the common good.

The Way of Commitment

A problem with the idea of commitment is that it suggests that commitment is "something" we can achieve. I can be committed to "this or that" way of doing things. On this level of achievement, our commitments lead us to act in both healing and destructive ways. A committed Christian may declare war or peace. Perhaps for our purposes here, we might think of commitment not as to this or that, but more as a commitment to "Being" itself; the times of our continued trying to be quiet, yet alert, as we listen for the voice of the Spirit which is within us. Such a way requires a determined, yet compassionate, will enmeshed in an attitude of faith and hope. The committed seeker is not above or beyond the human condition. Rather he or she is in the midst of it. Seeking God seems to require one to become increasingly immersed in his creation rather than withdrawn from it. It may be less a matter of whether or not we will lose our way than a question of countless times lost, of how we will find our way back. At the center of the committed life is the struggle for meaning and reconciliation. No better illustration of such struggle is that of Paul as described by William Johnston: "For this struggle is at the root of Paul's being—at the level of the self. Paul never sets himself above us; he never poses as the enlightened man; he never says that he has arrived. He is in the hurly-burly with the rest of us. And so in vivid words he describes the anguished struggle between the two selves at the depth of being. 'I do not understand my own actions. For I do not do what I want, but do the very thing I hate . . . I do not do the good I want, but the evil I do not want is what I do.' "[6]

So on we go, trying to become more fully human in what often appears to be an inhumane world. Seeker and non-seeker alike, the committed and uncommitted, all share the same foolishness that we refer to as "living" in all of its contradictory emotions. Still, at the heart of it, there is a difference. For the one not seeking God, there is the world in all of its neon glory. It is true enough that its beauty can intoxicate the senses, but it is after all only "skin-deep." For the committed seeker, there is something else, a special, secret place; the secret place where one can receive rest and nourishment in order to return to life's marketplace more vital than before to do the work one is to do. The solitary trips of Jesus to the desert or the beloved mountains, wooded valleys and strange islands of St. John, point the way to the special place: the place where the needs of the heart are brought forth in the light of the spirit, where the silence of the mountains enfolds the wounded spirit with healing and purpose. Such a secret place is both within and without us. We may become one with it so that no matter where we are, the special place is accessible. The key to that place is love and since we were first loved, the door always remains open through which we may enter. Jesus said, "Let not your hearts be troubled; believe in God, believe also in me . . . As

35

the Father has loved me, so have I loved you; abide in my love."[7] Perhaps in the final analysis, it may be that we are only able to see that which what we are committed to. Could it be that the One whom we seek has been with us all the time?

Critical Choosing

There are times in our lives when the choices that we try to make are of particular importance. A work or vocation to live and die by; a mate to explore the heaven, hell, and all that is in between of intimacy; and children to bear not only the grief of our own lost dreams, but also the hopes of dreams still to be born. At least as time passes each of us is inclined to become more mindful of the importance of these choices in defining our own personal meaning. It is through these times of critical choosing that the world sees us most clearly for what we are. Each morning's reflection from the bathroom mirror previews the judgment that the world may render regarding the value and meaning of our choices. The faces of our families and friends, even of our enemies, tell us more than we want to know about whom or what we are seeking. And, as always, the choices not made and the paths not taken teach us as much about ourselves as do the ones we have pursued.

Choosing one's life work or vocation may start on a more conscious level with the adolescent daydreams of years past. Long summer days when the possibilities for one's life work seemed as varied and endless as the slowly passing shapes of clouds. Yet as the time of choosing grew nearer, our dreams were challenged by the dreams of others. The burdensome dreams of parents who want a better life for us than they had, at least materially speaking. The seduction of romantic dreams where the rush of the heart challenges the logic of the head. Such dreams can become overpowering

36

when fused with one's emerging sexual energy.

Finally, there are the competing dreams of life-long friends that resist the threat of separating relationships that have for so long been inseparable. Questions concerning marriage, where to go to college, and what to major in become less clear as the dreams of others call out to be included in our own dreams. Somewhere in the process of translating our dreams into concrete realities, the possibilities for our life's work can become less clear and more confused. Somewhere along the way, the adolescent's creative dreams of vocation may become lost among the energizing demands of the road to material and interpersonal success. Instead of being called to a life's work, we choose a job. The voice from within calls to us and guides us toward a vocation that will not only earn us a living, but will also help us to become more alive. The ladder of the world's success often does not move in the same direction as the pathway to God's purposes. Frederick Buechner writes: "There are all different kinds of voices calling you to all different kinds of work, and the problem is to find out which is the voice of God rather than society, say, or the superego, or self-interest. . . . Neither the hair shirt nor the soft berth will do. The place God calls to is the place where your deep gladness and the world's deep hunger meet."[8] In other words, my life's work should be something that I am called to, a direction that I feel compelled to move toward in the deepest part of my being. Such a calling is an essential part of my spiritual integrity; an ongoing personal revelation of God's nature both within and without me. In addition, my life's work should serve the needs of my community. Both personal and communal, for better or worse, it is through my vocation that most people will know me for what I am. It is primarily through my work that I communicate to the world how I feel about myself and the God whom I am

37

seeking. Are my messages testimonies of hope, perseverance, and reconciliation or are they ones of despair and cynicism? Perhaps at times they are both. Perhaps, as with the struggle inherent in most choosing, it is a matter of degree. Nonetheless, for the most part, does the Spirit of God come more or less alive through me into the world and the lives which I touch? The life's work to which we answer will encourage or discourage our journey to God. It is never too late to dream again and follow that vocation in our seeking.

Romantic dreams hold forth a special promise of emotional and physical fulfillment. When in love everything seems possible and within one's reach. Little else seems needed other than the presence and attentions of the loved one. The raw emotional and sexual energy of adolescent desire bathes everything in its aura of urgency. Justice now! Freedom now! I want it all and I want it now! As a romantic seeker, I desire a passionate God from my own personal frame of reference who will waste little time in solving the world's problems. A problem with my adolescent need for a passionate God is the tendency for me to perceive myself as being the "center of the world" rather than being at the "center of his will." As such, my search for the Father can move no farther than the boundaries of my own personal history. As I grow in years, through grace I may be able to expand my dreams into a vision of a compassionate God who tempers his passion with mercy. And if I can hold onto such a vision, perhaps I too can grow toward such balance. The passion of the heart reconciled to the logic of the head can merge into a compassion of the spirit. Still with most of us, where affairs of the heart do battle with the mind's logic, the heart usually wins out. Such a victory is short in duration, but sweet in intensity. The shortness of the heart's season is itself a part of the Journey to God, signaling a passage of rite from the passionate promise of forever into the disillusionment of the here and now. This meta-morphosis continues toward the reconciliation of the forever and the now into the timeless heart of the compassionate Father. Simply put, "the heart is opened by being broken."[9]

There are those persons, however, who choose to try to resist the journey by clinging to romantic dreams, leaving little room or energy for enlarging their vision. For them, feeling in love becomes more important than being in love. The romantic myth is protected at all costs. Sam Keen puts such a dilemma in perspective when he states, "Romantic love lasts between ninety days and a year. In the harsh light of proximity, the illusion begins to fade. The gentleman turns chauvinist. The shining knight is really interested in conquest. The fair maiden is more chaste than caught; her magnolia heart conceals a manipulative will. Or both are romance junkies who must fall in love every three months to avoid both intimacy and the threat of being alone."[10] It seems important to choose one's life partner with both the heart and head; but since we often don't do so, perhaps a good marriage is more an act of God's grace than one of our own wise choosing. In any event, everyone wants a good marriage—one in which the partners are com-patible emotionally, sexually, and politically. To choose a life-mate is not a single critical choice symbolized by the marriage vow. Rather it is an ongoing process of choosing. One may be strongly attracted to someone and fall in love, an image that reflects the urgency of romantic dreams. Yet being "swept off one's feet" does not indicate the purposeful caretaking and com-mitment required for marriage partners to experience the full richness of intimacy. It is in the context of marriage that such nurturing seems to flourish most meaningfully. As a romantic, I may fall in love; but through a vital marriage I may grow in love. As Victor Frankl writes, ". . . even in love between the sexes the body, the sexual element, is not primary; it is not an end in itself, but a means of expression."[11] And better still, at some point in time such a marriage can remind me that, in a sense, I am not alone in my search. That where there was one, now there are two seeking the way to God. One could look at the marriage relationship as itself being a symbolic image of the Trinity —the three in one. It is a man, a woman, and their relationship. Each has an individual character and together they have a collective nature. The two persons who create the marriage relationship bring with them a potential for growing in love or falling out of love. Strong individual traditions impose pressure on the infant collective relationship—the marriage. Careful nurturing is required if it is to survive and flourish. Critical choosing continues to contribute to the evolution or dissolution of the trinity, for better or worse. Through grace, such choices may eventually allow the two persons to lose themselves to the fulfillment of their intimate communion—a fulfillment which points to something beyond themselves, yet which is realized in the midst of their most loving moments. It is from this grounding of marital love that we find the courage to extend love to others who themselves seem unlovable and more often than not reflect the frightened shadows of our own personal darkness. As our dreams are increasingly expressed through larger visions of community in work and in love, we move from a world for me to a world of us. The passion of the individual evolves into compassion for the group. "Within the ambience of the group, it is not intense passion that is valued so much as orderly care, not wild encounters with strange loves, but quiet kindness."[12] An important part of our contribution to the community's evolution—the group's journey to God—is to see that our participation does not end, that in its own way it remains connected to the eternal. We accomplish this through our children. Our children help us to keep intact not only our memories of the past but our memories of the future as well.

Children of the Flesh, Children of the Spirit

Each of us is a parent. Each of us has spiritual children. Some of us also have children of the flesh. The abused, battered bodies and psyches of children whose names are legion testify with silent stares that biological parenting may leave a pathway of blood and tears as well as provide a hope for the future. Pleasant memories and unspoken nightmares share the memories of many childhoods past. While some of us have children of the flesh, all of us, whether we like it or not, have children of the spirit. A smile or a frown, the whip or embrace, one's presence or absence, each in its own way prepares the children for the day they too will become aware of their life journey. Who among us cannot remember the teacher or grandparent or kindly neighbor who seemed to understand and accept us when no one else did, even those who were supposed to love us the most? Who cannot remember when we were children walking wide-eyed into the pain of experiencing betrayal from those persons closest to us? Each of us touches the lives of many children and makes a difference in their lives. More than that, we touch the child in the lives of all whom we come in contact with. Our children carry with them our sins and hopes. In their faces we see a reflection of the future—theirs and ours. Our vision may be a traditional one of doctors, lawyers, wealth, and power. Such a limited vision would be unfortunate for them and for us. Perhaps we can enlarge our own dreams in order to also make room for the dreams of our children, dreams that will allow them to hear and respond to the voice from within them as well as to our and other voices calling from without. It is worth remembering that "what the neighbors" or other persons think about our children may be less important than how they feel about themselves and, as a result, that they are more important than what they have.

The Pathway Continues

As seekers, our journey to God is an ongoing pilgrimage of choices and consequences, confusion and compassion, and grace and growth. Our continuing struggle to lose our ego-centered self-interests to the center of his will is enhanced by our commitment to a compassionate way and to the nurturing of the Holy Spirit who exists in the special place that is within each of us. The fruits of our journey are of the flesh and of the spirit as made self-evident through the significance of our relationships in work, marriage, and family. The pathway to God may be straight, but the route our kind chooses is often a winding, uneven way with enough dark corners to freeze the heart with fear and just enough light to taste the joy of what lies beyond. Still it is enough that we hunger for more; and although bruised, we continue the journey with a smile hidden in our hearts. The God who invites and encourages us to know him is a God in motion, revealing himself to us in ways both familiar and new; and his promise to us on our journey is not one of comfort, but rather one of meaning. As we make our way along the chosen paths of this life, we would do well to remember that our journey is not ours alone, but also everyman's. Our steps will not be the final steps along this way. The final steps will not be taken by us, but by others—our children of the flesh, our children of the spirit.

Endnotes

1. Victor Frankl, *The Unheard Cry For Meaning* (New York: Simon & Schuster, 1978), p. 30.

2. Victor Frankl, *The Unheard Cry For Meaning,* p. 34.
3. Frederick Buechner, *Wishful Thinking* (New York: Harper & Row, 1973), p. 77.
4. Matthew 26:39
5. Scott Peck, *The Road Less Traveled* (New York: Simon & Schuster, 1978).
6. William Johnston, *Silent Music* (New York: Harper & Row, 1974), p. 127.
7. John 14:1-2: 15:9.
8. Frederick Buechner, *Wishful Thinking,* p. 95.
9. Sam Keen, *The Passionate Life* (San Francisco: Harper & Row, 1983), p. 73.
10. Sam Keen, *The Passionate Life,* p. 72.
11. William Johnston, *Silent Music,* p. 126.
12. Sam Keen, *The Passionate Life,* p. 107.

4

SEEKING AND SUFFERING

"My God, my God, why hast thou forsaken me?"
(Matthew 27:46)
"Wither shall I go from thy Spirit?
Or wither shall I flee from thy presence?
If I ascend to heaven, thou art there!
If I make my bed in Sheol, thou art there!"
(Psalm 139: 7.8)

No matter which pathway we choose, suffering will be our companion and teacher for a portion of the journey. The broken heart of a love that was supposed to last forever, a broken body's response to the consuming fire of a dreaded illness, or the broken minds of dreams turned into dust, all point to the darkness of suffering's visitation. Whether or not we understand the purpose or meaning of our times of suffering, the experience is a living reality, one which shapes the nature of our journey to God. No one looks forward to suffering. Rather it is with an uneasy eye that we survey the landscape of our lives to detect signs of its unwelcome presence and take whatever steps we can to prevent or at least diminish its impact. Still, suffering waits on us patiently, taking whatever form it chooses to make its influence known upon our lives. A part of our suffering sleeps in the darkest corners of our hidden dreams, ready to be awakened at the appointed time when life's circumstances invite it into our personal experience. The possibility of the unthinkable encourages a sense of paranoia that a poem by Stephen Crane aptly describes:

> There is a grey thing that lives in the tree-tops
> None know the horror of its sight
> Save those who meet death in the wilderness
> But one is enabled to see
> To see branches move at its passing
> To hear at times the wail of black laughter
> And to come often upon mystic places
> Places where the thing has just been[1]

Is suffering to be limited to its potential for devastating human lives, whether dispensed randomly or by design? Is punishment its only name or does suffering have another side—a positive meaning?

Doubt and Despair

Doubt has two sides. There is the side that if allowed will persist in diminishing the joys, big and small, which are available to each of us. Am I a good enough parent? Am I performing adequately in my job? Does my wife or husband really love me? Does anyone love me? These and other questions while normal enough can inhibit the very qualities we are striving for if considered too narrowly and intensely. It is as if the doubt itself rather than the quality of life becomes the benchmark for who we are and what our life is about. It is certainly no secret that we live in an anxious age. Toxic waste dumps, famine, the homeless, in-curable disease, and the threat of nuclear war point to a world which often seems out of control and one which we have to a large extent made. Through action or inaction, our complicity in the state of the world can add guilt to our increasing sense of doubt. The world can become a dangerous land of shadows and I a victim silently waiting my turn with little or no hope in the future. In our modern secular age such a state of doubt is often labeled "depression," which Martin Seligman defines as "learned helplessness" or, for purposes of our spiritual journey, "learned hopelessness." The wall of doubt and depression which we may find ourselves against can easily enough convince our cynic's heart that there is absolutely nothing we can do about our dilemma. The narrow, rigid view of the cynic accepts only the worst possible outcome as reality.

As a result, even if the door to our prison is open, we do not notice as we plod through our lives, settling for survival in the illusion of a hopeless world, a world which we have helped to create. If on occasion through glazed eyes we see the possibility of a way out of our meaninglessness, we rely on our sense of guilt to discourage us from taking the chance. For no matter how bitter the taste of the life we have chosen, it is a taste we have grown accustomed to. And the known hell of our hardened hearts may be preferred to the unknown territory which lies beyond the wall of our doubt and depression, a wall carefully constructed of broken dreams and promises and the many names fear goes by. And on that wall our motto is clearly inscribed: "Always expect the worst and you will not be disappointed."

The dark side of doubt and depression leads us to a place of despairing souls where even the shadows are gone and only darkness resides. Having forgotten that darkness comes before the dawn, the despairing heart sees only a disembodied vision of the night; no illuminating stars, only blackness; and, as Stephen Crane states, it occasionally hears "the wail of black laughter." Despair is the consequence of a journey where doubt and depression are our primary guides, a journey with no future, a journey with no heart.

Left unchallenged, despair in the end can come to a point of denying life itself.

As stated earlier, there are two sides to doubt. Depression is not its inevitable expression. It has another feature: in our proudest, most self-righteous moments, it can bring us down to size. This side of doubt can help us reaffirm the important lessons found in humility and meekness, lessons that remind us that we do not control what life brings us but that through grace whatever life does offer can be experienced in a meaningful and often joyous way. And while our doubting can paralyze us, it can also move us. Such doubt can help us to continue refining the choices we make and the paths we take as we continue to seek relationship with God. Such refinement can be both exhilarating and sobering. To move through the darkness of doubt and despair into the transforming light of faith gives us hope. Yet the perplexing questions concerning the relationship between suffering and evil remain. So we go on about the business of living in the face of such unanswered questions, reminded from time to time in the senselessness of the world's pain that like Job we still want to know the answer to "why." We long to make sense of suffering and evil. At least a part of our effort to seek God is an effort to find answers to our and others' suffering.

Suffering and Evil: The Case of Job

Why does God allow evil and suffering to exist in our world? The fact that it exists is troubling enough, but the knowledge that each of us will sooner or later personally taste its bitterness and sorrow is even more frightening. We can protect neither ourselves nor our loved ones from the experience of suffering. The title of Harold Kushner's book, *When Bad Things Happen To Good People*, drives the point of our questioning even closer to home. It is unsettling enough

47

when bad things happen to bad people or for that matter, when good things happen to bad people; but when bad things happen to good people, where is the justice of it? The story of Job is the classic confrontation of good and evil within the context of suffering. Job was "blameless and upright, one who feared God, and turned away from evil." As a result, according to religious tradition, he ought to have enjoyed a long and successful life. Unfortunately for Job, as the story goes, he found himself in ruins, his land and cattle gone, and his children taken from him in death. As if that were not enough he had a terrible case of leprosy, had a less than understanding wife, and was pestered by three acquaintances who claimed to wish to comfort him. A good, virtuous man was reduced to a suffering shadow of what he had once been. Why? The three acquaintances held to the religious tradition of the day and contended that Job must be guilty of some great secret sin. Other traditions might suggest that such suffering in terms of evil is but an illusion and only exists in one's mind, or that perhaps it is a reality of reincarnation and Job was suffering not for evil rendered in his current life but for sins committed in another, previous life. Job, however, would have none of his comforters' speculation regarding his proposed secret sins nor would he succumb to his wife's suggestion that he go ahead and let go of life and end his misery. In the midst of his agony he defended his worthiness and questioned God's fairness. "He has put my brethren far from me, and my acquaintances are wholly estranged from me. My kinsfolk and my close friends have failed me; the guests in my house have forgotten me . . . I have become an alien in their eyes."[2] Job sat there in the middle of his despairing situation with sores and friends running from him and the memories of a life that had been transformed from a good dream into a living nightmare. He had little left to lose. His life, what there was of it, seemed to be almost over. Still he sat there, but not silently. All that was left of him continued to cry out for justice. Either Job was guilty or God was not just or, as Harold Kushner suggests, God was not all-powerful.

Much of the suffering in the world is irrational. The silent ovens of the concentration camps, the haunting eyes of the starving in Africa, the maimed bodies of Beirut's children, and the rubble of an Armenian earthquake all give witness to suffering's design on the world. Yet the senselessness of the world's suffering is not necessarily related to a senselessness of the spirit. Suffering in the world is not necessarily any more related to suffering in the spirit than the world's success is related to spiritual growth and meaning. How can the sixty-five-year-old double amputee student in my class, who lives at the local Veteran's Home, be so full of life and so eager to learn? One would think he was at the beginning rather than at the end of his life. Perhaps he is. How can the handsome student with the new sports car, caring parents, and everything in the world to live for be so confused and lost. One would think he was at the end of his life rather than at the beginning.

Perhaps he is. A person with an open heart and confined to a wheelchair, although severely limited in the world's terms, may move with ease and grace on the spirit's journey. Is the earthquake's ruin, the bloated belly's lack of food, or the weapon's wound evil in and of itself? Or is evil to be found in human response, whether it be the terrorist pulling the trigger or the apathetic person who switches off his or her heart to the problems of the homeless as easily as one switches off the television nightly news? What was the greater injustice that Job experienced, the loss of family and property or the response of his wife and friends? Are human beings and other life forms intricately woven into an ecological tapestry that interconnects a common destiny or is it everyone for himself? As Job and those around him were bound together by his suffering, each of us is connected to the suffering of those we live with and know of.

Job continues to live. He lives on the wrong side of the tracks, in the exclusive neighborhood, on death row, in the waiting room where the surgery was unsuccessful, and all the other in-between places the human heart hides. For some, the suffering in the world becomes food for the spirit's journey. For others, such suffering signals an attempt to postpone or withdraw from the journey. While we may not ever understand the "why" of suffering, asking the question deep within our own being can help transform us into greater intimacy with the One we seek. Thomas Merton says, "Prayer and love are learned in the hour when prayer becomes impossible and your heart has turned to stone."[3] The suffering of others and our own suffering can merge in a bridge of compassion which leads us to the heart of a God who suffers for his creation.

The Bridge of Compassion

As Jesus looked out over his beloved Jerusalem for one last time, the ignorance and indifference of his people washed over his own anguish into a compassionate outpouring of a suffering servant: "O Jerusalem, Jerusalem, killing the prophets and stoning those who are sent to you! How often would I have gathered your children together as a hen gathers her brood under her wings, and you would not!"[4] The suffering father who mourns the distance between him and his prodigal child is aware of the suffering he and his creation have to endure as the price of their relationship. Yet there is a bridge, a bridge of compassion, that can be traveled by mortal and immortal alike; a bridge that feels the prodigal's hunger and the pain of Job's running sores; a bridge that allows choices to be made in the mortality of the world or the immortality of the spirit. And at the center of our own suffering is the compassionate heart of the Father who is waiting for us. He can see us at the distance where we have chosen to be and he waits for us to come closer. Our unanswered questions lie at the center of his knowledge. But first we must cross the bridge of compassion which binds mortal and immortal together through life's times of suffering. Harold Kushner writes regarding suffering that we should ask "not where does the tragedy come from, but where does it lead to?"[5] Perhaps much of the evil in life is to be found in the countless times we choose not to cross the bridge; when we missed opportunities to enhance our spiritual growth and that of others. Standing at the bridge which offers mortal and immortal a chance for a fuller relationship, our hearts may close. When such a choice is made, feelings of potential awe and wonder may become instead feelings of fear and anger. The suicide or the homicide provide severe testimonies regarding the consequences of our inclination toward evading life's questions in favor of answers without vision or hope. A bridge not crossed can become instead a barrier, freezing the heart and paralyzing the mind to the spirit's possibilities. Can those of us who try to withdraw from our and others' suffering actually be successful in our efforts or are such attempts finally only another part of our journey to God? Can we truly play it safe in an unsafe world?

The Problem of Evasion

Scott Peck suggests that our efforts to avoid legitimate suffering is at the root of all emotional and mental sickness. He goes on to state, "Evil people resist the

51

awareness of their own condition."[6] As we continue to evade the choices that life's joys and tragedies offer us on our journey, our evasion spins an ever greater and more intricate web of deceit, a web that prevents the heart within from engaging the world without. Perhaps nowhere is such evasion more apparent than with our efforts to deny death. Elizabeth Kubler Ross writes, "It is the denial of death that is partially responsible for people living empty, purposeless lives; for when you live as if you'll live forever, it becomes too easy to postpone the things you know that you must do."[7]

We become the stranger in a strange and dangerous land. Number one becomes the only one. The reflection in our mirror provides the limits of our hope and the boundlessness of our despair. Full of fear and danger, we want a sense of security and peace without having to make the difficult choices that seeking God requires. To put our predicament in more secular terms, we "want the self-confidence of adulthood without having to grow up."[8] We want to master life's possibilities with a credit-card personality; enjoy now and pay later, or preferably don't pay at all. Contrary to such desires, an authentic journey to God requires that we pay as we go. Still, through our evasiveness we try to conceal who we are and the debt we owe. Words and gestures conform to the fashion of the day, whether such fashion is formed by the United Way or by the United Klans of America. Perhaps even our evasiveness, a detour though it may be, is itself a part of our journey. Life with all of its joy and sorrow enlarges our world as a part of God's revelation to us, a continuing revelation of possibilities which we must choose to respond to. Sometimes we choose to work through the experiences life brings us. On other occasions, we try to evade experiences we perceive as being difficult.

Memories of God's touch and scent in the past

52

often fade before the glimmering lights of my own present ambition. In my young adulthood I translated my search for God into a search for the wisdom of the world. My God became a fashionable God clothed in philosophical, religious, and social trends, and most importantly, in my own search for acceptance and status. The wonder and awe of childhood and adolescent questioning about God's role in his creation eventually became reduced to questions regarding my role in my own creation of reality. Questions about God were often lost within my own answers. My sense of oneness with God on a mountain-top starry night seemed to disappear in my attempt to negotiate a corporate merger with him, one in which we were partners. With my graduate education behind me and the resulting enlarged ego in front of me, I came to think that it was up to me to solve the problems of the real world "for" God. Through a mixture of both genuine efforts and evasiveness I eventually came to see the holy sciences more clearly than the Holy Spirit. I no longer felt the earlier need to be subservient. There no longer seemed to be much reason for me to struggle with the need to remain open to God's Spirit, since we were now partners. Now I could do it for God and for Me. As my priorities became increasingly mistaken for God's priorities, I assumed that his priorities were often out of fashion. Such awareness required that I continue to increase my role in solving the problems of the real world. The agonizing questions of an eternal Job became whispers as the ambitions of my not-so-distant past awakened to the trumpet call of the world's reality— a religion of success. However, with success there is never quite enough of anything . . . except fear. Of course, fashion can provide a temporary hiding place. Clothes and plastic surgery can hide one from aging, and a new car or job can mask a feeling of failure or inadequacy. Even prejudice, when in style, can elevate a poor self-image at the expense of someone else. The problem with fashion is that it can easily lead me away from the central force of my journey to God, the center of my inner life in favor of my outward appearance which often seems more relevant to the world's reality. As a result, I may become more visible to others at the expense of my own personal inward sense of vision. I may become more the center of attention outside as I attend less to my center inside. Sam Keen writes, "Instead of seeing, we will seek to be seen . . . to be is to be seen; I only exist as a reflection of the opinions others have about me; if I 'lose face' I lose myself."[9]

In a world where only winning and success really count for anything, fear finds its place in the center of my being. Perhaps it is as Sheldon Kopp states, "You can run but you can't hide."[10] Perhaps it is necessary that on more than one occasion I go down the path of greed, ambition, and self-deception in order to learn that there is no rest on that road. When we try to hide from our fear, we feed it instead, and in the end we find ourselves the victims of our own greatest atrocities. Peering out from behind our hardened hearts, the person we have lost seeks solace in a place we have forgotten. When all finally seems lost, we somehow recapture a faint memory of a special place. And the place we find ourselves once again is at the foot of the bridge of compassion. And like Job, after all the advice and torment the world has to offer, we must choose again whether or not to use such experiences to seek God. The memory of that bridge is the standing invitation offered by the One calling us to relationship, a relationship that makes who we are and can become worth the price that is paid. Yet, the invitation is one that we are free to refuse and we often do. The invitation continues both in our failures and successes, when we are hiding and when we are open. As Kopp suggests, we may for a time be able to evade the truth and hide from ourselves, but mercifully not from the One who loves us most.

We may finally come to a point where we realize that we are more than what our eyes and minds see, more than blood relations and a few close friends, more than competitors in a struggle of us against them. We may begin to understand that we must also learn to see with our hearts. It is only through our heart's vision, both broken and open, that the cruel illusion of our separateness from each other can be overcome. With the passing of our body's season our spirit can continue in community, not limited by time and space, but as part of the continuum, of a living reality—a bridge from our moment in time to the timeless moment.

From Suffering to Significance

Suffering is both universal and relative. All of us eventually experience the loss of loved ones and personal injuries. Yet two similar events of suffering may have dramatically different outcomes, depending on how the two individuals in question respond to them. For one person, the response to a debilitating injury might be a profound awakening to what is important in life, a significant increase in his or her quality of relationships with others. To another individual, responding to the same injury may result in a withdrawal from life, a closing of the heart and journey into despair. While we may never understand the nature of suffering to our full satisfaction, we do eventually come to know that there is only one way out. The way out is the way in. And that way is the way to God. To find our way to God, we must not withdraw but rather struggle to keep our hearts open so that we can find the courage to cross the bridge of compassion. Through such a crossing, our anger and fear can be transformed into humility and wonder. Job's anger and frustration directed toward God melted into humility when he was confronted with the reality of God. "Then the Lord answered Job out of the whirlwind: who is this that darkens counsel by words without knowledge? Gird up your loins like a man, I will question you, and you shall declare to me. 'Where were you when I laid the foundation of the earth? Tell me if you have understanding.' "[11] The answer to Job's questioning was not found in the wisdom of the world. The answer was found in Job's humility in the presence of God. As the story goes, God rewarded Job many times over what he had lost because of the persistence of his faith and his steadfastness. His wealth and health were restored to him in a bountiful way. For some, the story's ending is the high point: from the strength of Job's spirit to the strength of his financial position by way of God's grace. Still, standing with Job as he surveys his vast expanse of fertile lands, one must wonder if there is not more than a hint of sorrow for what was lost: the laughter of his children and the comfort and confidence of his wife. Yet there he stands, viewing the magnificent, if uncertain, promises of the world which God has laid before him. For me, the high point of Job's story was when he was down and almost out; when covered by sores and hanging on by a thread of his stubborn faith, Job could still say, "Behold, he will slay me; . . . yet I will defend my ways to his face."[12] What if God had not rewarded Job in the end with the wealth and promises of the world? What if there had only been stillness—a deafening stillness? Somehow I believe Job, suffering and determined as he was, would have hung there by his fragile, stubborn thread of faith, affirming his love for God and protesting the injustice of it all. And I believe God would have come to him as he does to each of us, not at the end of our suffering bearing gifts, but in the midst of it bringing the gift

56

of himself. The gift of God's presence is the gift of love, a gift that transforms our and Job's suffering into a timeless dimension of significance, a moment's memory that meets us on the bridge of compassion as we find our way to God.

Endnotes

1. Stephen Crane, *The Complete Poems of Stephen Crane* (Ithaca: Cornell University Press, 1972), p. 134.
2. Job 19:13-15
3. Spiegelman, A. and Schneider, B. (Eds.), *Whole Grains* (New York: Douglas Links, 1973), p. 106.
4. Matthew 23:37
5. Harold Kushner, *When Bad Things Happen to Good People* (New York: Schocken Books, 1981), p. 137.
6. Scott Peck, *The Road Less Traveled* (New York: Simon & Schuster, 1978), p. 280.
7. Elizabeth Kubler-Ross, *Death: The Final Stage of Growth* (Englewood Cliffs: Prentice Hall, 1975), p. 164.
8. Scott Peck, *The Road Less Traveled*, p. 305.
9. Sam Keen, *The Passionate Life* (San Francisco: Harper & Row, 1983), p. 60.
10. Sheldon Kopp, *If You Meet the Buddha On The Road, Kill Him* (Palo Alto: Science & Behavior Books, 1972), p. 166.
11. Job 38:1-3
12. Job 13:15

5

THE SEARCH FOR
SOMETHING MORE

*"Jacob left Beer-sheba, and went toward Haran.
And he came to a certain place, and stayed there
that night, because the sun had set. Taking
one of the stones of the place, he put it under
his head and lay down in that place to sleep.
And he dreamed that there was a ladder set
up on the earth, and the top of it reached to
heaven; and behold, the angels of God were
ascending and descending on it!"* (Genesis
28:10-12)

Our times of suffering, in all their forms and expressions both physical and emotional, point us toward a
greater sense of humility and compassion. As we learn
to listen more carefully to these lessons, we begin to
realize that authentic joy and meaning are not necessarily related to the successes of the world in which
we live, that perhaps we may be able to experience
the "peace that passes understanding" during both
the peaks and the valleys of our days. Such a realization invites us to dream the dream of Jacob. A growing
sense of compassion allows us to have Jacob's sight
as we begin to have visions of the transcendent possibilities of heaven's staircase. Jacob's dream encourages

us in our search for something more by proclaiming the realities of the future which are found hidden in the present, the purity of the God we seek found hidden in the trusting innocence of the child we love, or the cleansing of heartfelt sorrow found hidden in our concern for the misfortune of someone we thought was our enemy.

As with the angels who are both ascending and descending the staircase, we are put in touch with the continuity of our life's time: the past, present, and future, each distinct in the limited perspective of our mind's eye, yet joined in the transcendent timelessness of a greater reality. It is through this greater reality that we find the special moments—the something more—that bring us closer to the God we seek. It could be said that we live all the days, hours, minutes, and seconds of our lives for these special moments, these magic moments when the light hits just right on autumn leaves or the smell of old wood and coffee mingle in a certain way with the evening breeze to recreate a forgotten memory. The mass confusion of so much of our lives gives way in those all too brief moments of awareness— of being known in place and time. Being at peace, if but for a moment, is a wonderful and unexplainable experience of grace that stands out of time's tradition; where color, light, smell, and touch come together in a particular way to lift us up and pull us into the heart of a greater reality than we can ever fully understand or comprehend. Is it real or is it a dream? Perhaps it is both. Perhaps it is the place where dream and reality meet. The early morning mist is the veil through which we see enough of the sunrise to dream of what it must be.

A Compassionate Vision

To experience the dream we need to nurture a sense of compassionate vision within our own hearts and minds. A compassionate vision gives us a taste of the transcendent, the ability to be fully present and aware of what is immediate, yet also simultaneously aware of the larger, more inclusive picture of the staircase from the present to the future. Jesus put it another way when he encouraged his followers to be in the world but not of the world. Paul's transcendent experience on the road to Damascus proved to be his "staircase" experience. As a result he turned from a narrow legalistic vision bent on persecution to a vision of compassion committed to the greater reality he had so dramatically encountered.

The compassionate vision is the lover's vision, a vision well acquainted with joy and despair and the range of emotions that fall in between. First love and first heartbreak and a lifetime of second chances give direction to our journey and an opportunity to go our way not only as love's explorers but also in community. Being wounded and knowing the healing that comes afterwards and being wounded again and having yet another chance for love's resurrection, keeps us close and together in the body of Christ, the reconciling reality of wholeness. We may think about and discuss the varieties of love: the philia of loving friendship, the eros of emotional and physical bonding (and in some cases unfortunately, bondage) and the unconditional agape love of giving for its own open and hidden joys. However, it is the last form of agape love, the no-strings-attached loving, through which the other forms can transcend the limitations of their human hosts. We experience such a transcendent empathy perhaps most readily with our loved ones. Their pain becomes our own as does their joy. It is a place we meet together in loud protest or in quiet, with tears or with laughter. Such empathy opens our hearts to include others, even the "least of these," even our enemies.

A compassionate vision broadens our search for

God to include all that is the mystery of life. The unspeakable joy and what seems to be the unbearable pain stand together. The questions of life which demand answers not easily found, if they can be found at all, sit quietly in the bedrock of a thousand human experiences, just below the topsoil of the world's answers, continuously being challenged by the storms of life. A compassionate vision is a reconciling vision; a witness to whatever is going on, good or bad, in both time and place; and using the experience of the moment as still another opportunity, another chance, to get closer to the One we seek. Through the window we see a star shining brightly a million miles away and our vision becomes the hope that joins us with that which we seek in a moment's passing. The spirit of our love and longing overcomes and transcends the space that separates us from the One who is love.

The compassionate, reconciling vision through the lover's eyes in time comes to see all that is life, all that has been created and is in the process of being created, bathed in the light of the Beloved. Our memory of what it was like to be young and in love and of the accompanying passion through which we perceived life's possibilities, gives us an example this world offers that points to the compassion of the greater reality. The journey from passion to compassion may not be an easy one; but it is one which if we struggle to keep our hearts and minds open, can lead us through a fullness of grace to the love that we seek. Still, such a vision is not a prize that once won becomes a trophy to be admired. Rather, a compassionate vision must be carefully nurtured day by day, experience by experience. And while the transcendent beauty of the early light of a coming day is a sight to behold, the neon glare of the world's light holds forth an incessant illusion of answers, not questions; of certainty, not mystery. A compassionate vision helps us to stay more keenly aware of the inner light, a light that encompasses the sun and the moon and the something more—a beacon light that keeps us in touch with the second-chance nature of our journey. Again and again our experiences bring us to the bridge of compassion; and each time illusion calls us back from the bridge, warning us of its dangers while the unknown invites us ever onward.

The Mirror of Illusion

The temptation of Christ in the desert mirrors our temptation: the gilt-edged power of the world in exchange for our feeble pledge of loyalty, a full belly in exchange for an empty heart; and if, tempted as we are, we say No to those two generous offers of the world, a challenge for us to at least put our money where our mouth is. Is our faith one of strength or fear? Are we willing to jump down from our fragile personal theology to test the God we seek? Should we call God's bluff as our own is called? Should we pass-the-buck? We could jump from a rooftop, drink strychnine, or even put our family's future on one roll of the dice in Las Vegas. After all, if God is there, let us demand that he prove himself. And we do just that as we long and pray for promotions, personal vengeance, and other assorted favors associated with our own rather than God's will.

As with the evil queen in the fairy tale, *Snow White*, the living of our lives begs the question, "Mirror, mirror on the wall, who's the fairest of them all?" And we hang onto the mirror image of our empty heart's vanity for all that we are worth. Having "laid up our treasures in this world where moth and rust do corrupt," we attempt to deny moth and rust as we cling to our attachments, our idols of success and power. In clinging to our illusions, we become side-tracked from our journey to God. The window to heaven we sought becomes nothing more than a mirror image of our own self interest, substituting a pretty smile for a loving one, information for wisdom, political power for personal integrity, and a passion for the temporary instead of a compassion for the eternal. The illusion of our own neurotic reflection leaves us empty and scared and looking for something— anything—to fill in the missing pieces of our lives. We may look to the television evangelists for superficial, quick pick-me-ups without requiring any deeper commitment from our own lives. Like our televisions, we can turn ourselves on or off to such experiences according to our mood or whim. We may look to religious habits for security; perfect attendance at Sunday School, never missing our daily Bible readings, or just acting morally proper. As committed to such habits as we may be, we fail to realize such habits alone are never enough; their focus on appearances, on keeping score, may have little to do with what is going on inside us.

Does our perfect attendance at church include our awareness of what is being taught and are those teachings, with the help of the Holy Spirit, being taken to heart? Are our daily Bible readings being done so that we can proudly bear witness to our having read the Bible through or are they more than readings? Are they meditations which nourish and guide throughout the good and bad days of our lives? Gertrude Nelson describes the dilemma of our confusing illusion with the greater reality of God's will: "In place of the periodic holy fast, we have become slaves to our perennial diets. In exchange for 'carrying our cross' in the constructive suffering that every life requires, we complain of low back pain. The old taboos, which we think we are freed of, crop up as new varieties of superstitions, and we take another vitamin. The neurotic is religious material done unconsciously."[1]

Unfortunately, the church, the institution created

to help us maintain an appropriate orientation in our journey to God, itself often supports the larger illusion of culture's tradition rather than the unorthodox and unlimited possibilities of the Holy Spirit. It often seems that the church as a religious institution is to a large extent the world in sheep's clothing. Is our church more the instrument of the Holy Spirit helping us to define our journey, or is it more the instrument of our culture, attempting to domesticate and confine the Spirit and keep spiritual pilgrims in the pen of tradition. Marcus Borg writes, "We live in Babylon often declared to be Zion."[2] We may worry and wring our hands about world hunger, but how often do we volunteer to help with preparing meals for the homeless in our community? Does our church spend more time with building and fund-raising, growth-oriented programs or with truly non-profit direct service ministries to those who are in need? It is worth remembering that the largest church is not necessarily the church with the largest heart or spirit.

Jesus, the itinerant preacher, saw through heaven's window and Caesar, ruler of the world, saw only the mirror's reflection. Which one do we choose, the mirror or the window? In a documentary on Mother Teresa by Richard Attenborough, Mother Teresa is asked time and time again by reporters, dignitaries, and others what her Sisters of Charity are actually doing? Her response was always the same: "Come and see. Come and See" . . . and do.

Over time, it becomes evident that passion alone is simply not enough. The passion for justice can too easily become the passion of hate and prejudice; the joyous passion of the Christmas congregation can too easily become the vengeful passion of the mob. It is through the eyes of the other and with the help of the Holy Spirit that our hearts can open to a transcendent sense of empathy and our passion can be transformed into a compassionate vision. Then, with Mother Teresa, we can move through the mirage of the world's illusions to a place of truth. We can "come" to the greater reality of the moment and "see" the truth found in the moment's place, and realizing through the grace of the Spirit what we need to "do," begin doing it.

The Search for Truth

Harry Truman, known as "give 'em hell Harry," once said, "I never give them hell. I just tell the truth and they think its hell."[3] The place of truth is not a resting place. It is not primarily a place where one's spent energies can be replenished. Yet at the same time when seen through the eyes of a compassionate heart, it is a place where strength and freedom are found. The search for truth is an everyday search and truth is found or lost in every nook and cranny of human relationship and experience. While most of us struggle with the truth hidden in all the conflicts and crises swirling around us each day, there are some spiritual pilgrims who stand in the place of truth. The place they abide is like the calm in the center of the storm. The winds blow; yet they remain calm and steady because theirs is a compassionate vision and they have "ears to hear" the spirit's song within the noise of the storm.

Jesus said, standing before Pontius Pilate, "For this I was born, and for this I have come into the world, to bear witness to the truth. Everyone who is of the truth hears my voice."[4] Abiding in the center of truth's experience, Jesus speaks clearly to our Pilates' hearts. Unfortunately, we often do not have the ears to hear. We want to know "about" truth rather than experience it. The world of illusion encourages us to keep our distance, analyze and objectify the nature of truth rather than open our hearts to its call. The raw simplicity of faith's pull toward truth does not fit well with the commercial packaging of the world's illusions. The search for truth is beyond the pretty and the ugly and the rich and the poor. Still, attractive illusions continue to offer us life's "something more": an improved love life if we purchase the new car, finer friends if we serve a finer wine, and fewer cares resulting from fewer cavities if only we will buy the toothpaste endorsed by more dentists. However, it is as Gertrude Nelson suggests, "We make a mistake when we believe, 'Lo he is in . . . the toothpaste.' The transcendent is illusive and nothing we package, shelve, or trade on."[5]

The transcendent "something more" we search for in order to move closer to the One drawing us ever nearer is fueled by the truth we hold in our hearts and express through the living of our lives. This truth is found only in relationship with the Holy Spirit and the others we live with in community. Each person we come into contact with in our community is an invitation to enlarge our vision. Through each "other" we come nearer to the "Other." However, a world where competition is preferred over cooperation makes it difficult for us to hold onto the truth. With the world's illusions, there is no "truth in advertising." We compete for success—to be number one. Yet in truth, in our heart of hearts, we can never be number one through competition. The success of the world is not likely to be translated into the wisdom of the Spirit. Competition separates us into "A" and "F" students, millionaires and paupers, offenders and victims—whatever the labels—us and them. At truth's center there is no us and them. We are all the body of Christ, the greatest and the least. The eyes of competition blind us to the greater reality that we are all number one. In our world of second chances, there are no second place finishes. In truth we participate rather than compete in community. And in community we are joined, the murderer and the saint and all that lies in between, along with the air and the water and the land in a continuing revelation toward God. Sooner or later, time and again, each of us, a representative of the whole, can choose truth or illusion, greed or generosity, light or darkness. Each struggle is everyone's struggle as together we make our uneven way toward God.

The body—our bodies—possesses millions of feet to "come" and eyes to "see" and ears to "hear" and hands to "do." It is through truth's transcendence that while retaining our sense of personal identity, we can at the same time enlarge our vision and see the big picture. Through the eyes of compassion our personal identities can extend into the reality of all that is alive. Truth is the meeting place of the mortal and immortal which unites all of life in the spirit of love. Love is the central element of truth and is the only power which can transform the world's illusions into meaningful lessons for our journey to God. The power of love in a community of relationships can open each of us to truth's liberating influence; an influence that allows us to not only more clearly hear and speak the truth, but to stand in truth—to live in its liberating presence.

It does seem easier at times to deal only with fragments of truth, using them as a means to distance ourselves from others rather than being united in a transcendent spirit of love. During such times, we may worry about losing our sense of self-control and fear others will see through our pretense as we stumble along the edge of our lives trying desperately to maintain a semblance of the image by which we want others to know us. Yet at the same time our deeper fear— the one that gnaws at us and keeps us scrambling— is that once others see us for what we really are, they won't care. We may even be able to recognize the truth and speak it, but still be unwilling to include ourselves within its compassionate sphere of influence. Whether we try to totally ignore truth or recognize and speak it articulately, we still find ourselves caught in an existence of half-truths, not sure of which way to turn—only sure of our commitment to evading its birth pains in our own hearts and being. Even in our most evasive times, truth continues to show its face to us. And sometimes it is only when, like Humpty Dumpty's, all the king's men cannot put our pieces back together, that we are most likely to feel its reassuring embrace. How many times when after days, months, or even a lifetime of evading the truth hidden in our hearts, of playing cruel games with each other, two people who used to love each other come to the bottom of the well that was their relationship to find that, exhausted and battered, they can finally be in truth with each other; they can finally begin to care again. It is during such times that the living hell of my past can be transformed by a moment's truth into the hope of heaven's possibilities. It is not enough that I recognize the truth, I must also act upon it—be obedient to it if I am to experience the transcendence of a love that transforms all that is past and all that is to be into the timeless dimension of God's grace. From such transcendence comes a living awareness of the grace of the greater reality that "makes all things new," that sets you and me free. Parker Palmer writes, "Only in obedience to truth can freedom be found."[6]

At this point in our journey, the question arises: how can we learn to become more obedient to the truth? How can we learn to keep our hearts and minds open to the quest for truth in a spirit of love? The answer is that wherever we find ourselves we must begin to nurture a personal sense of spiritual discipline through practice. Practice may not make us perfect but it does give us a spiritual grounding which can help increase our ability to remain open and growing through all the experiences, both good and bad, that life brings to each of us. Such a practice is prayer.

Endnotes

1. Gertrude Nelson, *To Dance With God* (New York: Paulist Press, 1986), pp. 12-13.
2. Marcus Borg, "Jesus and the Kingdom of God," *The Christian Century*, April, 1987, p. 380.
3. *The Sun*, 131. 1986, p. 40.
4. John 18:37
5. Gertrude Nelson, *To Dance With God*, p. 16.
6. Parker Palmer, *To Know As We Are Known* (San Francisco: Harper & Row, 1983), p. 65.

6

THE PRACTICE OF PRAYER

"And I will pray the Father, and he will give you another Counselor, to be with you forever, even the Spirit of truth." (John 14:16-17)

"In the higher part of the contemplative life, a man is above himself and under his God." (The Cloud of Unknowing)

Starting in ancient times, prayer was put into the process of our journey to allow us the opportunity to maintain a relationship with the One we seek. Prayer encourages us to keep our journey in perspective and lets us ask for and receive help along the way. In our own way, we have to learn how to pray and what to pray for. And even though we will make mistakes, it is important for us to accept on faith that every prayer is heard and answered in ways that are in our own best interests, whether we fully understand the answers or not.

As in the art of communicating with each other, the art of communicating with God falls victim to our human inclination to talk more and listen less. Marriage, child-rearing, and work-related problems inevitably find a common denominator in the painful consequences of not listening, of not being more fully aware of what is going on around us, of not hearing what the other is saying in terms of words, body language, and in other more subtle, intuitive ways. With spouses, parents, and co-workers we are usually more interested in giving direction than in receiving instruction. As a result, we tend to talk past those persons we are trying to help or, even worse, we often end up talking to little more than a mirror image of ourselves. The consequence of such an orientation is that the end result of taking action to solve a problem not fully understood, is no solution at all. Instead, it creates yet another layer to the existing problem, making final resolution even more difficult. Listening and speaking, then, is a basic problem in our communication with the other, whether the other is our child, spouse, fellow worker, or our God.

Speaking Prayer and Listening Prayer

It is important for us to realize that a fundamental rule in seeking God, in experiencing the transcendent "something more," is that we learn to fully listen before we speak or act. Fully listening includes all our senses—sight, hearing, taste, touch, and smell—brought to bear on a given problem or context in the fullness of our minds' and hearts' abilities—in an intuitive spirit. Such spiritual intuition encourages a sense of reverence and openness in our preparation for response to the challenge that awaits us, whether it be the crown or the cross. Needless to say, learning to listen isn't easy. The world calls for immediate action, the spirit says be patient—listen. The world demands that we take charge of others; the spirit encourages us to surrender to the will of the Other. The world says, "I did it my way"; the spirit says, "Not my will, but thy will be done."

Petitional Prayer

It seems no accident that of the five basic types of prayer (petitional, intercessory, confessional, thanksgiving or praise, and the prayer of quiet), the one involving our speaking to our own self-interests, our own will, is the type of prayer we most frequently use. We can safely assume that petitional prayer maintains its number one status on the prayer chart. While any prayer made with an open and genuine heart is an important part of our spiritual journey, it is easy for petitional prayer to narrow itself to a wish list more compatible with the world's illusions than with the purposes of the God we seek. If you will just help me get this promotion . . . if you will just not let this loved one die . . . if you will just help, let, make, do—whatever it takes for what I want or think I need to come to pass, I promise to do this or that which always amounts to being a better husband, father, son, daughter, wife, and, of course, Christian. Whether politely asking or desperately demanding, we are often inclined to try to influence God's will with our own. And like small children, when our wishes aren't granted, we often slam the door to our hearts shut and sulk in the shadows of our own misguided dreams. In a poem about his dying brother James Autry poignantly describes the echo of everyone's prayer of petition:

> Against all those desperate prayers
> whispered in airplanes
> and hospital corridors
> Against all those deals and bargains
> of new beginnings and new behaviors I thought God
> could not afford to pass up
> Against all the wild promises
> he died anyway.[1]

72

With each petition unanswered and unfulfilled on our terms, dreams scatter and the personal sense of our own mortality comes acutely into focus.

Intercessory Prayer

Intercessory prayer also has its place in our official religious life. Unfortunately our intercessory praying is likely to be more global than personal. Help my church to make a difference rather than help me to become aware and act on what I can do to make a difference. Help world hunger to be eradicated rather than help me to find the courage and willingness to serve on a local soup line for the homeless. Help my friends to get through the pain of their divorces rather than help me, although embarrassed and not knowing what to say, meet my friends in their pain and reassure them with my presence. It is too easy for us to forget or evade the truth that God is more likely to intercede through us rather than independently of us. The surgeon's steady hand, the friend's compassionate courage, the stranger's cup of cool water, each may represent the hands, feet, eyes, and heart of the living Christ. Too often like petitional prayer, when we ask God to intercede on behalf of someone, we are really asking God to see it our way and intercede according to our best advice. Help my friend to see how much she hurt me and how wrong she is so that she can repent, or help my friend's pain to be relieved so that he can be returned to the way things used to be. Do we pray for what's best for our friend according to God's purposes, or do we pray according to our own desires? Do we pray for God to alleviate pain and suffering or do we pray for the courage that through us, God can help us do our part to fulfill his will in the midst of pain and suffering?

Confessional Prayer

Like the other forms of prayer addressed here, our sense of confessional prayer often includes a hook or two. When are we most inclined to confess? What do we perceive as the purpose of confessional prayer? When our sense of guilt and frustration over some wrong we have committed becomes too much for us to bear and we have run out of energy and schemes with which to solve it, we turn to God; and as if saying "uncle," we confess what's in our hearts—we tell the truth for a change. Of course, we are not telling God anything he doesn't already know. By telling the truth to him, what was a wall separating us from his love and grace is transformed into a bridge through which we can come into a fuller relationship. By confessing and confronting the lie, our evasion of the Other turns the power of truth into a liberating opportunity in our world of second chances. Many times we feel that a consequence of our confession is an obligation of God to grant us our wish. In such instances, confession becomes little more than petition's smoke screen. Like the small child relating to his or her mother, on such occasions we say, "I'm sorry, God; I did it; now can I go out and play." The cleansing of confessional prayer offers us as much as anything, the emptying of our burdensome attachments—our fear and anger—through which we gain access to a compassionate vision, a vision which gives us the eyes to see a new day and the hope once again for a fresh start.

Prayer of Praise or Thanksgiving

Another often neglected aspect of confessional prayer lies in its often being associated only with confession of wrongdoing. However, telling the truth to God has another liberating side. The prayer of thanksgiving or praise is also confession. The typically human thing to do seems to be to take credit for our good fortune and assign responsibility to someone or something else for our misfortune. However, the practice of confessing praise and thanksgiving is an important part of our prayer life for it helps us keep our life in a clearer perspective. "The car was wrecked, but thank God, my family is all right," or "Thank God for the grace of a loving if imperfect family," are examples. And even in the midst of our greatest misfortunes, confessing praise for the love of the One who never passes away has within such a prayer its own quiet liberation. With Job, we are invited to pray, "Though you slay me, yet will I love you." Why do terrible misfortunes bring some persons even closer to God while such tragedies devour others in the despair of a darkness with no hope of deliverance? While the answer to such a question can never be fully understood, it can be experienced. Whether Job or Jesus or the little old man next door or the prisoner on death row or the small child in the cancer ward, a spirit of wonder and thanksgiving can itself, like perhaps nothing else, embrace the timeless invitation, born on the wings of hope from the One who is love.

The Prayer of Quiet

In one way or another, the forms of prayer previously examined are "speaking" prayers. Through the sounding of our words or as thoughts in our minds, these heartfelt expressions represent our efforts to significantly contribute to relationship with the God we seek. Yet we might ask ourselves, "what about the 'listening' part of our prayer life?" If I am doing all the talking—always taking the active role in communicating with God—am I prepared to hear him when he is taking the active role or speaking to me? Do I really possess a listening heart that is receptive to God's message? Am I willing to take the time to really listen to him, to be truly quiet in order that I may better hear the still small voice? Perhaps I should also be concerned with the actions I take in my life which are based more on my speaking to God than in listening for his voice. It is as if I tell God all my troubles and concerns, thank him for his time, and then decide for the both of us what I should do about those concerns. And when the action I take doesn't work out, I wonder why God let me down. This approach to prayer and to our relationship with God reminds me of a story wherein a man was on the roof of his house during a flood. When a neighbor in a boat came to rescue him, he refused, declaring that he wasn't leaving and that he had a steadfast faith that the Lord would rescue him. The flood waters continued to rise and the man found himself clinging to his chimney. A rescue helicopter approached him and dropped a rope ladder on which he could climb to safety. Though sorely tempted, he refused once more, indicating that his faith was still strong and that God would still save him. After the man drowned, the scene shifts to heaven. The man's first question to God was, "Why didn't you save me?" God's response was to the point: "What are you talking about? I sent a boat and a helicopter." As this story illustrates, a basic problem in our prayer life as it directs us along our journey to God is that we often choose not to let it direct us. We don't consistently prepare ourselves to listen to our heart of hearts from which the will of the One we seek calls forth.

We need to learn to listen before speaking, a problem which is apparent in our relationships with each other and with God. The prayer of quiet, our listening prayer, provides the foundation upon which our speaking prayers come to have more meaning and purpose. An old French peasant, reflecting on prayer several hundred years ago reported, "I don't say anything to God. I just sit and look at him and let him look at me."[2]

Just sitting and looking and opening ourselves to be looked at . . . and waiting; waiting to find God, waiting to find ourselves. Looking through the eyes of our heart to find ourselves in God and the God we seek in ourselves. And like the old peasant of Ars, sitting together, saying nothing, doing nothing, just being together on the bridge of compassion, illuminated by the love we seek, by the love which has found us . . . and binds us together as one.

Listening and speaking, the two basic elements of communication, are important; yet they are not enough. We seek something more. We seek the transcendent something more that Thomas Merton described a few days before his death: ". . . the deepest level of communication is not communication, but communion. It is wordless. It is beyond words, and it is beyond concept. Not that we discover a new unity. We discover an older unity . . . We are already one. But we imagine that we are not. And what we have to recover is our original unity. What we have to be is what we are."[3] How do we work through the veil of our imagination's attachments and, recovering our original unity, find ourselves in a living community with God? One significant way is the way that is beyond words and concepts, the way of the prayer of quiet which is also popularly referred to as meditative prayer.

As important as meditative or listening prayer is to the nature of our spiritual journey, it is not without its own potential for seduction and corruption. Popular psychology has extensively documented the physical and mental benefits of relaxation training and breathing exercises which are secular variants of more ancient meditation traditions. However, as we seek deeper levels of experience on our spiritual journey, the stakes become higher than an improved tennis game or less stressful job performance. We can find ourselves in a no-man's land somewhere beyond the psychologically well-adjusted consumer, yet far short of unity with the One we seek. In such a place, the siren's song of corruption can become sweet music to our ears, encouraging us to become attached to our special feelings of something more that such prayer may bring, rather than continue seeking the wordless reality that is beyond even feelings. Our spiritual enthusiasm can easily outdistance our spiritual maturity, and this can place us in a dangerous in-between place and time. When we choose to be our own guide in the meditative experience, it is once again all too easy to confuse our voice with God's voice, our will with his. Thomas Merton describes the contemplative seeker who mistakenly thinks he is listening to God, but instead is listening to the empty promises of his own limited vision: "He trusts his own visions. . . . He identifies the will of God with anything that makes him feel, within his own heart, a big, warm, sweet interior glow. The sweeter and the warmer the feeling, the more he is convinced of his own infallibility. And if the sheer force of his own self-confidence communicates itself to other people and gives them the impression that he really is a saint, such a man can wreck a whole city or a religious order or even a nation. The world is covered with scars that have been left in its flesh by visionaries like these."[4]

If we are to follow Merton's advice and beware of the sole authority of our own interpretations and perceptions of listening prayer, what are we to do? Perhaps we could follow Micah's advice concerning what the Lord requires: ". . . To do justice, and to love kindness, and to walk humbly with your God.[5] A love of justice, kindness, and humility represent essential fruits of those seeking God throughout the pages of the Old and New Testaments as well as on the living pages of today's testament. While these qualities may be the desired fruits of our labor, we still long for a more immediate, living authority to help guide us. Recognizing the limitations of our own filters through which we experience feelings and thought, we may even turn to the counsel and guidance of other seekers whom we respect and consider wise in the way of prayer. Still, as helpful as such a response may be, it is not enough. If not my own guide or the guidance of other fellow pilgrims wiser than I, then who? There is really only one answer. The answer we seek is a gift from the One we seek, the Holy Spirit —both guide and comforter, leading us toward that from whence he came.

The Holy Spirit As Guide

It is through speaking and especially listening prayer that we embrace the Holy Spirit and become increasingly aware of that place in us now that was before we were and will be after we are. The historical Jesus lived two thousand years ago; the Holy Spirit lives now. Through the Holy Spirit, then and now come together in a timeless tapestry of evolving experience. Without the Holy Spirit, we are left to our own devices and an ancient history lesson. Access to the Holy Spirit alone opens our eyes to a greater transcendent reality, one which can both transform us and transport us to the God we seek.

Jesus said, "If you love me, you will keep my commandments. And I will pray the Father, and he will give you another Counselor, to be with you forever, even the Spirit of truth, whom the world cannot receive, because it neither sees him nor knows him; you know him, for he dwells with you, and will be in you . . . it is to your advantage that I go away, for if I do not go away, the Counselor will not come to you; but if I go, I will send him to you."[6]

Jesus knew that even among those followers closest to him that some degree of the world's confusion still existed. The world demanded a Caesar, not a servant; a palace, not a stable. His days as Counselor and Comforter in the flesh (but of the Spirit) were drawing to a close. It was a bittersweet time, a time to wean his followers and us from misplaced expectations and the anxiety of abandonment. As he modeled for them and us his own life, each person has to do his or her own work, respond to his or her own calling and keep the faith as best he or she can, doing the will of the One who sends us and calls us home. Jesus promised us a guide, another Comforter and Counselor, to encourage us along our way. "The Counselor, the Holy Spirit, whom the Father will send in My name, he will teach you all things, and bring to your remembrance all that I have said to you. Peace I leave with you; my peace I give to you; not as the world gives do I give to you. Let not your hearts be troubled, neither let them be afraid."[7]

Once we begin to understand the possibilities of the promise of Jesus, we come to the point of wanting the Holy Spirit to be in us and with us. Yet the question remains, how do we gain increasing access to the One we seek through the Holy Spirit? How do we become more aware of the Holy Spirit who is with us and invite him into the intimacy of our hearts? For some of us, it may be a radical awakening. Like Jonah, we may be dragged kicking and screaming into the service of the Spirit; or like Paul, we may experience something on the "road to Damascus." Many others of us may experience a gradual awakening, like the flowering of a tree in springtime. Whether radical or gradual, once we have become awakened how can our relationship with the Holy Spirit be maintained and developed? According to the Scripture, Jesus says, "If you love me, you will keep my commandments."[8] The answer to gaining and maintaining greater intimacy with the Holy Spirit seems to be one of obedience, yet perhaps not obedience as the meaning has popularly come to be known. Obedience appears to often mean simply, or not so simply, following rules, laws, precepts, or guidelines with little or no questioning. Such obedience may range from trying to faithfully live by the ten commandments of the Old Testament to the New Covenant of Jesus to the rules of a given Christian denomination or even to being a good Republican or Democrat. However, the root meaning of obedience seems to have largely been lost along the way to modern living. The Latin root word of obedience is *ob-audire*, which means to hear or to listen. Obedience essentially has to do with our willingness and capacity to listen to the voice of God through the Holy Spirit as well as to the needs of each other. That is why listening prayer or the prayer of quiet is so important. It prepares us to obey the requirement for experiencing the truth Jesus frequently ended his stories and teachings with: "He who has ears to hear, let him hear."

We cannot think or talk our way to a relationship with the Holy Spirit. We first have to learn to listen in silence in order to understand and complete the work we are supposed to do, the work that moves us along our way to God. With the help of the Holy Spirit, we are allowed to experience and be changed by transcendent reality. The burning bush Moses witnesses becomes more than a bush that is burning; the suffering of Job becomes more than pain and loss; the blindness experienced by Paul on the road to Damascus becomes more than a physical disability. Each of these persons listened to the possibility of the impossible and experienced the presence of God's mystery, a presence that changed their lives in powerful ways. This, then, is the purpose of prayer and the opening of our hearts to the Holy Spirit; that we can more fully experience the something more, the transcendent possibilities of the greater reality toward which we journey.

Prayer is our primary way to stay more centered in the place of truth which is so important to our maintaining a clear vision for our journey. We need to remember that although invisible, given the weight of our world's worries, a small prayer's genuine effort or even a heartfelt thought of really wishing someone well, can provide the missing spark that ignites the fires of hope; the fires which can warm a single, solitary heart, or melt the barriers which separate members of a family who have become strangers, or open the minds of a prejudiced community. From a flicker to a flame, to a fire consuming separateness and hopelessness, yet warming the heart and igniting the will of a confused and hungry world. From the one to the many, from a feeling to a thought to an act to a visionary attitude. It all starts with the still, small voice, a flicker or a whisper; a fleeting memory of a greater reality waiting to become incarnate through us in our world, right here and right now.

Endnotes

1. James Autry, *Nights Under A Tin Roof* (Oxford: Yoknapatawpha Press, 1983), p. 88.
2. Jill H. Adels (Ed.). *The Wisdom of the Saints* (New York: Oxford University Press, 1987), p. 35.
3. Neil McKenty. *In The Stillness Dancing* (London: Darton, Longman and Todd, 1986), p. 100.
4. *The Sun.* 131, 1986, p. 40.
5. Micah 6:8
6. John 14:15-17; 16:7
7. John 14:26-27
8. John 14:15

7

COMING HOME

"But while he was yet at a distance, his father saw him and had compassion. . . . But the father said to the servants . . . let us eat and make merry; for this my son was dead, and is alive again; he was lost, and is found." (Luke 15:20-24)

We can never quite forget the feel and smell of home, even if we have never really felt at home. We still have imagined how it would be. Home sweet home. Home is where the heart is. Childhood memories. Sacred memories. Memories, particular and selective though they may be, help keep us together in the midst of life's craziness. An image of a home remembered— or if that isn't possible, at least a home hoped for—keeps us going in the ups and downs of our adult lives. Sunburned and exhausted, we find that the summer vacation, like life itself, finally winds down the road to the place from whence we came. The house from which we were so eager to escape for a few days or weeks comes instead to be the home which we long to return to, a place of security and comfort, a place we know and where we are known. Maybe that is what our lives are really all about—our search for a home where the welcome mat at the entrance has our name on it. Not Joe's, Sue's, or Abraham Lincoln's, but our own name carefully and forever etched, a special invitation that welcomes the me that is unique into the equality of community that is us.

Perhaps we are, all of us, prodigal sons and daughters, good and bad, trying to find where we belong. Who knows, maybe it is all part of the plan. The fast-track career and the good deal we negotiated with the salesman at the store may both just be ways, sometimes desperate ways, we try to create hope for ourselves on our journey to God. Maybe if the deals are good enough, we can somehow, through grace, come to feel good enough about ourselves not to deal at all and begin to feel at home with ourselves. Of course, it isn't likely to work that way. That is why Jesus said, "It is easier for a camel to go through the eye of a needle than for a rich man to enter the kingdom of God."[1] Maybe that's also why it wasn't until the prodigal son ran out of money and the world's answers that he was finally able to find his way home. Like him, we have to do two things: Remember the peace and security of the place from which we came, even if it seems mostly like a dream, and act on the faith of that memory. Coming to grips with who we are and what we are about is also a part of our coming home. Honest self-appraisal and genuine questioning encourages the compassion of the Holy Spirit who guides us homeward.

The Witness

A nine-year old heart was once broken and opened to the injustice of innocence betrayed through a crucified Jesus. The brokenness created an opening through which the Holy Spirit made itself known. The timeless witness of the Spirit to love's sacrifice

84

as the price for renewal was more felt and recognized when understood in the deepest part of the child's being. The mystery of that moment transformed the child's journey into a conscious one. And while that consciousness was avoided as the child-becoming-adult addressed other interests and needs, the witness of the Spirit remained, from time to time penetrating the young man's evasiveness just enough to prod or encourage him along the path. Such is the presence of the Holy Spirit in a life. Sam Keen writes, "God is always incognito, hiding on a busy street, in falling rain, caressing us in every breath, in our DNA, encouraging us to become who we are."[2]

The Holy Spirit is also referred to as the Spirit of Truth. The Spirit bears witness to the truth; not necessarily to what you and I want to see as the truth, but rather to things as they are. The God that we seek is the One who sees us as we are and loves us as he does all of creation. And the only place we can meet God is the place of truth. We know and are known in that place. "Not only do I invest my own personhood in truth and the quest for truth, but truth invests itself personally in me and the quest for me. . . . The known seeks to know me even as I seek to know it; such is the logic of love."[3] And the translator of love's logic, our guide to the place where we and the One we seek can meet, is the Holy Spirit.

As the Spirit's witness helps us along our journey, we find we must become less attached to the world's answers and offerings. We stay involved, yet we become increasingly less of the world. The idea of letting go is not an easy one to follow. More fully accepting that our journey is one of living out the questions of life rather than finding answers is no easy task. Yet that is what is required. "Not my will, but thine" is easy enough to say, but difficult to do while being in the world. Our inclination is to "make things happen" rather than to "let things happen." Two people can make physical love, yet we have to let love in its fullness happen. The passion of physical love pales in comparison to the compassion of partners who have grown in love over the years, becoming one in spirit as well as flesh. As with the relationship to our spouse, the relation to our life's journey must also unfold, must be revealed in its own time. We may try to make a career for ourselves in this or that profession, yet in reality we don't build careers or lives. Instead, we respond more or less to the unfolding of our lives.

In our coming to identify more closely with the Spirit's witness, we find we can more freely let go of the illusion that we are in charge of our lives and begin to respond to whatever life brings us. And remarkably we find as we lose ourselves to the Spirit's unfolding, we begin to find our way more clearly than when we tried to do it our way. Of course, there are still struggles and detours. Coming home is a life-long journey. So we begin again. Still, something is different now. Our starting over times no longer start over from the beginning, but rather start over from the places we find ourselves stuck in. And we come to see more clearly that the beginning is where we are headed.

Reconciliation and Synthesis

Love and hate, fear and courage, and joy and sorrow often pull us in opposite directions and point to the state of contradiction we often find ourselves living in. We hate because we don't feel adequately loved. We take courage not only in spite of but also because of our fear. Our sorrow blinds us to the joys that lie waiting to be recognized in the extraordinariness of our ordinary lives. We may find ourselves torn and bleeding in experiences that seem to offer only extremes; all or nothing. The wildly swinging pendulum of our perceptions of life keep us moving, but with little sense of direction. We expect so much of ourselves and one another. The husband who expects his wife to make him feel loved; the wife who hides behind the courage of her husband; and the sorrow of the lover, rejected twenty years ago, now rejecting the offering of friendship from the small boy with frog from next door. Each of these persons (including the part of them that lives in each of us) expects the other to make him or her complete, while denying or evading his or her own responsibility in relationship.

There are no spectators in the dance of life. Each of our dances may be different; some faster, others slower; some of us may even be dancing alone. But dance we must, for the movement itself, no matter how erratic, is a part of our journey. The flailing arms of the abusive parent and the contortions of the victim-child are locked in a dance of pain and sorrow no less significant than the magical dance of the loving elderly couple who move in harmony as one.

An important part of our journey is getting in step with the rhythm of life. Just as there are natural seasons by which crops are planted and harvested, each one of us has a personal rhythm with its own seasons. Becoming more sensitive to the seasons of our own personal rhythm can help us to become more open to the larger rhythm. And with the help of the Holy Spirit we can begin to experience more clearly the heartbeat of that rhythm which calls us home to the One we seek. Heart to heart, we can come to more fully experience our journey. W. Paul Jones writes, ". . . each person has times approaching ecstasy and days of desert blues—of new moon and full moon. To identify these . . . and flow with them in the Spirit's leading can be to sacralize each person's unique spiral around the forward life pilgrimage."[4] The question could be asked, How do we become more sensitive to our personal rhythms so that we can begin to experience reconciliation and synthesis as we journey into the heart of God?

The central theme of getting in step with the dance that is the rhythm of life is one of repentance. It requires us to continue in our efforts to turn away from the promises and loyalties of the lesser values of the world and toward the value of the all-encompassing love of the One we seek, which forgiving us, enables us to forgive ourselves and others. The struggle to forgive leads us toward reconciliation. A forgiving heart restores the pendulum's balance and rhythm. As the balance returns, we can begin to understand that our journey is not all or nothing, but rather all "and" nothing. The coming together of all and nothing leads us into the heart of the Christ, reconciling the world unto himself. From a winter's emptiness of the crucifixion through the resurrection, comes the seed of a spring's hope. And what connects and reconciles the two events is the forgiving love of the Father through his Son. "Forgive them father" . . . becomes "Invite them Father." "From my death to your life . . . and I will be with you always even unto the ends of the world."

The reconciling power of a forgiving love enables us to realize that our life's journey is not just a journey of success or failure, love or hate, courage or cowardice. Such a power encourages us to respect our times of cowardice and fear so that somehow with the help of the Spirit, newfound courage is born from their season. Reconciliation allows us to honor our failures rather than attempt to deny them. Paying our respects to such experiences invites wisdom's compassion to help us to take heart instead of losing hope. Through reconciliation we find ourselves more open to the lessons of the Spirit's witness. And as a result, what once tore us apart and separated us from our fellow pilgrims and the path we sought, now through the

Christ's forgiving love and our response of repentance, integrates rather than separates us. The resulting synthesis helps us see the way more clearly and gives us strength for the journey. Black and white, male and female, parent and child, lost and found, all and nothing become one in Christ. Frederick Buechner writes, "Out of Nothing he creates Something. Out of the End he creates the Beginning. Out of selfness we grow, by his grace, toward selflessness and out of that final selflessness, which is the loss of self altogether, 'eye hath not seen nor ear heard, neither have entered into the heart of man' what new marvels he will bring to pass next."[5]

The Prodigal Returns

At the beginning of this chapter, we considered that the prodigal son had to come to a place in his life where he looked beyond the answers of the world in order to become open to the love of his father which called him home. The love that called him home as it does to each of us has always been there. We are all prodigal children coming from different places and traveling in different ways, yet all seeking the same destination. We know all too well that a home can express the chill of a tomb or the warmth of a manger. Yet the destination we seek is one that reconciles the two; that reconciles all differences. And after all our wanderings, all the peaks and the valleys of the world outside and our hearts inside, we finally begin to realize that what we are coming home to is the part of ourselves that never left home. As our journey unfolds, we begin to sense that while there are miles to travel still, the love that calls forth to us is in us. We were created in the image of a God that is love. And although we may for the time being see that image only "through a veil darkly," we see enough of it to know that it is where we belong; that

it is the only place we will ever truly feel at home. T. S.
Eliot writes:

> "We shall not cease
> exploration
> At the end of all our exploring
> will be to arrive where we started,
> Knowing the place for the first time.[6]

At the end of our journey that is what awaits us;
that we will know as we are known. And as if for the
first time, we will join with the ancient One we seek
in the place that is love.

So the journey continues and sometimes we get
afraid and want to stay put; we even want to stop
looking or have the journey end. But we go on any-
way, bright-eyed and sad-eyed, lightly or as if we
were carrying a great weight. Still, we continue on
the journey, even looking forward to it as it lies waiting,
just around the next bend.

Endnotes

1. Matthew 19:24
2. Sam Keen, *The Passionate Life* (San Francisco: Harper &
   Row, 1983), p. 210.
3. Parker Palmer, *To Know As We Are Known* (San Francisco:
   Harper & Row, 1983), p. 58.
4. Gertrude Nelson, *To Dance With God* (New York: Paulist
   Press, 1986), p. 13.
5. Frederick Buechner, *A Room Called Remember* (New
   York: Harper & Row, 1984), p. 13.
6. T. S. Eliot, *Four Quartets* (New York: Harcourt, Brace &
   Company, 1943), p. 39.

www.ingramcontent.com/pod-product-compliance
Lightning Source LLC
Chambersburg PA
CBHW071103090426
42737CB00013B/2444